AUDREY HEPBURN
INTERNATIONAL COVER GIRL

AUDREY HEPBURN
INTERNATIONAL COVER GIRL

SCOTT BRIZEL

TITAN BOOKS

AUDREY HEPBURN: INTERNATIONAL COVER GIRL

ISBN: 9781848566118

Published by
Titan Books
A division of
Titan Publishing Group Ltd
144 Southwark Street
London SE1 0UP

First edition October 2009
10 9 8 7 6 5 4 3 2 1

Text and compilation copyright © 2009 by Scott Brizel.
Individual covers copyright by the respective magazines.
The magazines represented in this book are from the
collection of the author. Photographs by Jay Dixon.

Visit our website:
www.titanbooks.com

Did you enjoy this book? We love to hear from our readers. Please email us at readerfeedback@titanemail.com
or write to us at Reader Feedback at the above address.

To receive advance information, news, competitions, and
exclusive Titan offers online, please register as a member
by clicking the "sign up" button on our website:
www.titanbooks.com

A CIP catalogue record for this title is available
from the British Library.

Printed and bound in Italy.

TABLE OF CONTENTS

6

INTRODUCTION

Film, Fashion, and Magazines

FILM, FASHION, AND MAGAZINES HAVE LONG BEEN intertwined, with each enjoying a complicated and shifting influence over the others, and each contributing in its own way to the creation and celebration of celebrity style. Until the American film industry matured in the 1920s, popular ladies' magazines had been the exclusive augurs, arbiters, and publicists of movements in fashion. As early as 1830, *Godey's Lady's Book* had connected women by providing a common forum for information, assistance, and advice about home-making issues. After the introduction of the sewing machine in 1846, the magazine substantially expanded its coverage of making clothing for oneself. Several magazines of women's clothing and style appeared in the United States by the 1850s, but *Vogue,* launched by New York publisher Arthur Baldwin Turnure in 1892, was the first to market cosmopolitan on-site fashion reportage as "news" to socialite and suburban house-wife alike. Among the sites showcasing couture innovations early in the modern fashion era were the theatrical stages of the 1890s (upon which even antiquarian dramas were presented entirely in prevailing Victoriana) and France's pres-tigious racecourses after the turn of the twentieth century.

Vogue's first issue made plain its aspiration to distinguish itself as a magazine for "society," not the average home-maker. An editorial claimed its domain to include "the cere-monial side of life . . . its particular phases, its amusements, its follies, its fitful changes. It may be a dinner or it may be a ball . . . the magnetic welding force is the social idea." In its first twenty years, *Vogue* mirrored the habits, leisure activi-ties, social gatherings, places frequented, and clothing worn by the "four hundred," the elite four hundred New York social aristocrats who were invited each year to the Astors' winter ball at their Fifth Avenue mansion.

A change in both tastes and coverage came with World War I (1914–1918), when a number of major couture houses closed in France—then the undisputed capital of fashion. Austerity came to override fashion's appetite for voluptuous whimsy and high-style exotica. In danger of losing its *raison d'etre* with the dearth of fashion activity during the war, *Vogue* rallied late in 1916, altering its editorial direction to emphasize speculation and prediction over mere observation and comment. This adjustment caught on with *Vogue's* colleagues and competitors, and after the war, when the floodgates of fashion reopened, this predictive direction for fashion-oriented print media became one of its most vital functions. With fashion's new boom and an ever-broader panorama of styles, the fashionable public sought more editorial guidance.

Film, emerging as an international medium at the same time, was able to display its images on huge screens to huge audiences, and so create tastes and establish trends. Through the studios' golden era, until television began to dominate in the 1950s, American film emerged as the primary media influence on fashion's mainstream.

After trying unsuccessfully to distinguish their products through trademarks and story lines (an early Metro ad of 1916 proclaimed: "It isn't the star and it isn't the play—it's the

BIOGRAPH COMPANY

ELEVEN EAST FOURTEENTH STREET

NEW YORK, N.Y.

May 21, 1910

Miss Betty Blayne,
    San Francisco, Calif.

Dear Madam:

        Replying to your letter of May
16th, we regret to state that we are not
issuing photographs of the artists com-
prising our stock company. We are
therefore returning your check for $2.50
enclosed with your letter.

                Yours very truly,

                BIOGRAPH COMPANY

L. E. W. — D.   L. E. W.
Enc.

In the early days of film, production companies had not yet fully recognized or capitalized on the influence that the images of their performers would come to hold over their audiences.

name [Metro Pictures] that guarantees you a fine evening's entertainment"), pioneering production companies shifted strategies when they discovered that audiences distinguished films by stars. Recognizing the commercial value of promoting certain contracted performers within their stock companies, producers broke from the early film tradition of uncredited performances and began to feature and promote certain actors. The first such promotion took place in 1909 via industry trade press, such as the *New York Dramatic Mirror.* The following year, Kalem Studios issued a poster of its actors for theater lobbies. Later in 1910, an early affiliate of Universal Studios was the first to identify a star through a publicity stunt (a false report that Florence Lawrence, a recent acquisition from Biograph Studios, had been killed in a car accident). It became apparent that the advent of performers as "stars" was the most important development in film advertising, and soon carefully crafted images became the focus of Hollywood's publicity machine.

The studios quickly evolved two separate units within their publicity departments, one for promoting the individual films through posters, press books, lobby cards, and such, and a second concerned with maintaining star images. By mid-decade, the surge of requests for pictures and biographical information for such stars as Mary Pickford, Lillian Gish, Mabel Normand, Fatty Arbuckle, Tom Mix, Norma Talmadge, and Douglas Fairbanks led to a flood of studio-independent "screen fan" magazines. The first, *Photoplay,* debuted in 1910, and it was followed quickly by others. The rise and golden age of the studio era in the '20s through '40s was driven in part by the star system, in which studios would promote and foster certain actors and actresses that they held under contract to burnish the star and the studio's brand. Screen magazines

such as *Photoplay, Modern Screen, Silver Screen,* and *Motion Picture,* mainstream lifestyle magazines such as *The Saturday Evening Post,* (the original) *Life, Ladies' Home Journal,* high fashion magazines such as *Vogue* and *Harper's Bazaar,* and local newspaper *Sunday Magazine* supplements all played parts.

Stars' influence on fashion proved invaluable to the film industry, which was able to forge a partnership with fashion and news magazines. The stars' prestige promoted the sale of magazines and fashions; magazines and fashions, in turn, enhanced the reputations of stars, with couture, to its profit, the style police. A synergy was born. Among the film stars of the '20s and '30s whose studio-cultivated styles penetrated into print media and fashion influence were Louise Brooks, for her timeless bob; Mae Murray, for her "bee stung" lips, which were a rage with flappers; Clark Gable, for his suave moustache; Marlene Dietrich and Katharine Hepburn, the former for her stylized woman's tuxedo, and both for breaking the look of women wearing trousers.

But by the mid 1950s, both French couture and Hollywood fashion began to cede their influence to the inexorable rise of television and the cultural dominance of youth, with print media increasingly in the foreground. It was in this context that Audrey Hepburn arrived in popular attention in her U.S. film debuts *Roman Holiday* (1953) and *Sabrina* (1954). Although she has come to be best remembered for her connection to haute couture, herimage in these first films was more significantly based on her characterizations of youthful vitality and emotionalism. In both films, she presented a combination of formality and casualness, sophistication and naiveté, reserve and impulsiveness. This versatility felt fresh and inspiring, and seemed a way forward along the unfolding societal transition toward later, more informal beatnik, mod, and hip youth cultures. The press around Hepburn's early career portrayed her as the inaugural icon of a new type of sex appeal, one that emphasized elfin spriteliness and youthful glamour. The following superb example of this by Ellis Whitfield from *Why? The Magazine of Popular Psychology,* February 1955, features a quasi-beatnik ode to Miss Hepburn in the bebop hip-speak of the day:

> *The nice thing about a good-looking doll, as Mr. Damon Runyon might have observed, is that she takes you out of yourself. Such good-looking girls as Mrs. Joseph DiMaggio nee Marilyn Monroe, and ex-Mrs. Frank Sinatra nee Ava Gardner, transport a lot of harassed American males into an earthy but irresponsible dream world, a sort of Big Rock Candy Mountain cum sex. Now, a new phenomenon has turned up in the field of fantasy: the actress who takes you out of the world altogether.*

> *Three such young ladies are currently around, all of them identifiable by their sprite-like haircuts, their elfin eyes, and their long supple legs. One is Jeanmaire, who was recently seen on Broadway in* The Girl In Pink Tights. *Another is Leslie Caron, who has graced a number of motion pictures. The third is Audrey Hepburn, a young lady who first impinged on the American consciousness in a comedy called* Gigi, *then wowed the customers with a movie called* Roman Holiday, *and finally was perfectly cast as the sub-aqueous Rhine maiden in a fable named* Ondine. *She now is to be seen in* Sabrina Fair.

> *In the bebop phrase, these girls are all real cool. They conjure up visions of dalliance among the planets, or in a crater on the moon, or 20,000 leagues under the sea. They are taking the psychological escapist (and who isn't, occasionally?) out of*

his mythical taxi and putting him into a space ship. The sexy sirens of Planet Earth still have their followers, but a good many men who last year were content to dream of a short trip to a no-baggage hotel with Marilyn or Ava would now like a weekend on Venus with Audrey.

> *Miss Hepburn does not give the impression of being untouchable, either in the water or in outer space. She just looks a little too good for the accommodations on land.*

> *Why, the reader may ask, should the combination of coals-and-seaweed prove so alluring to the male? What's the matter with the girls who look hot-eyed for here instead of for Mars? Well, nothing, really. Except if one is going to use sex symbolism as a fantasy device to escape the Hydrogen Age, why not take a long trip? A few years ago, before the pressures of our society became quite so intense, it seemed enough to escape reality for a few hours. These days the idea of swimming around in space, perhaps for eternity, with Miss Audrey Hepburn seems pretty attractive.*

Though it had been her youthful charm and exotic beauty that inspired the first wave of journalists to write about her, Audrey's subtler characteristics contributed to her becoming a notable clothing designer's muse. Couturiers ascribe inspiration to the physical characteristics of their models as well as their interior qualities—a certain inner poise and hard-to-define complexity of character. Self-awareness, natural instinct, and (perhaps hard-won) experience all help such muses bear the mark of a self-styled original.

Hubert de Givenchy has said of Audrey, "She was capable of enhancing all my creations. And often ideas would come to me when I had her on my mind . . . it was like that from the start . . . Audrey had a big personality . . . she always knew what she wanted and what she was aiming for . . . In the choice of her dresses, in wearing them with such elegance, chic, and simplicity . . . her style was born as we now know it: the sophisticated sheath, the shoulder grazing décolleté, the full skirt, a scarf tied around her head and the pillbox hats. . . . In a very personal way, she created her own look—'The Hepburn Style.'"

Haute couture, literally "high sewing," is a term that originated with custom-made clothes, whose production was centered in France for the first hundred years of modern fashion beginning in the 1850s. In the late nineteenth century, upward social mobility and increased demand gave rise to a less formal and ceremonial brand of couture for a still rarified but more general audience. However, couture at the highest level was still designed with a specific woman in mind to complete the fashion, fulfilling her vision of or aspirations for herself.

The more generalized couture, while not designed for a specific individual personality, was nonetheless created to project a persona (sophisticated, self-assured, artistic, and so on) that would become its aspirational selling feature. At the still less rarified and more accessible levels of fashion, mass production and off-the-rack, the garments are created with still less personalization. The individualization at this level comes through the selection and combination of elements. Ironically, although haute couture is recognized as art, because it involves the vision of an accomplished designer, style (the act of an individual's personal selection and combination) is the enterprise that marks the consumer's unique expression and creativity. While fashion is of obvious importance to magazine editors, style is more important to individual expressiveness, and more enduring, given fashion's inherent mania for change.

"Style is independent of fashion," wrote *Vogue*'s editors in "Spotlight On Style" in September 1976. "Those who have style can indeed accept or ignore fashion. For them fashion is not something to be followed, it is rather something to be set, to select from or totally reject. Style is spontaneous . . . the unpremeditated . . . divine gift . . . of the few."

Audrey was celebrated by fans and by editors of fashion, film, and style magazines (then and now) not just because she seemed in some way to complete and embody the spirit of the haute couture fashions designed for her, but because she had an inimitable sense of style—of personality bringing fashion to its highest level. She had a strong and independent eye for style, often incorporated options from among contemporary fashions, and, in fact, often worked with her wardrobe designers to finish ideas and sketches to suit her taste. As eight-time Academy Award–winning costume designer Edith Head observed, "Audrey could have been a designer herself, she had such perfect taste."

As a performer, clothing was very important to Audrey, because she believed that she wasn't a good enough actress, always insisting on this point, despite winning the Academy Award very early in her career. Audrey had admitted to journalist Whitney Williams for Canadian *Liberty Magazine* (March 1963) that she was so inclined to be preoccupied as she threw herself into a character, that sometimes between camera takes she would go directly to her dressing room without so much as glancing at someone waiting to talk to her. "I can't chat between takes," she said. "I'm not a good enough actress. I can't turn it off and on like others can. If I lost the feeling for the part I'm doing, I haven't the ability to call it back. Only with hard work, concentration, and effort am I able to achieve a standard that might qualify me as an actress. But certainly I'm not yet a good one."

Effective wardrobe gave Audrey the conviction to transform believably into character. "Clothes, as they say, make the man," she said. "But they certainly have, with me, given me the confidence I often needed." Of Cecil Beaton's "absolutely divine" ball gown for *My Fair Lady:* "All I had to do was walk down those stairs. The dress is what made me do it. . . . What has helped me a great deal with the part are the clothes. It was often an enormous help to know that you looked the part; the rest wasn't so tough anymore. In a very obvious way, let's say you do a period picture, whether it was *War and Peace* or *The Nun's Story,* where you wear a habit. Once you're in that habit of a nun, it's not that you become a nun. But you walk differently, you feel something. That is an enormous help. And also, in modern-day pictures wearing Givenchy's lovely simple clothes, wearing a jazzy little red coat and whatever little hat was then the fashion—I felt super."

The history of couture glows with partnerships of muse and designer: Joan Crawford and Gilbert Adrian, Grace Kelly and Edith Head, Carole Lombard and Travis Banton. Audrey Hepburn brought such inspiration to Hubert de Givenchy, who, in his own words, "had the pleasure of making all her clothes, not only for all her contemporary films, but also for herself." Part of Audrey's appeal and great gift of inspiration for the designers and couturiers with whom she worked was of course that she was beautiful, but beyond that, she became so great a muse because she embodied self-possession, depth, and balance of character. As the daughter of Dutch Baroness van Heemstra, Hepburn was authentically of the aristocracy, with regal comportment further emphasized by ballet training and European cultural experience. However, these gifts of grace and breeding were tempered by extreme hardships during her developing years.

Audrey's complexity of character is a recurring theme in attempts to capture her essence in words. Photographer Cecil Beaton described her in the pages of *Vogue* in 1954 as, "Intelligent and alert, wistful but enthusiastic, frank yet tactful, assured without conceit and tender without sentimentality." She balanced femininity and tomboyishness, youthful energy and mature composure, informality and refinement, humility and hauteur, and offered an innovative personal style trademark that continues to inspire designers and entertainment and fashion editors, who feature her image in books and periodicals around the world.

Audrey's Early Years: Childhood and the War (1929–1947)

AUDREY HEPBURN'S EARLY EXPERIENCES LAID THE foundations for the qualities that designers and fans would find so appealing in her character and image: graceful inwardness, but also confidence and ballast.

Audrey Kathleen Ruston was born on May 4, 1929, in Brussels, Belgium. She was the daughter of a Dutch mother and Anglo-Irish father, and thus officially a British citizen. Audrey's mother, the Baroness Ella van Heemstra, twice divorced, had two sons when she married Joseph Victor Henry Ruston, also divorced, a diplomat in the Netherlands East Indies.

In May 1935, after years of quarreling, Joseph left his wife and six-year-old daughter. He afterward never attempted to contact them. The terms of the divorce stipulated that Audrey be educated near London, and she was enrolled in a small private school in the village of Elham in Kent. Reportedly, Audrey was shy, awkward in mixing with other girls, and inclined to overeating and nail biting. She eventually discovered her lifelong love of dance by way of lessons in a dance school run by the six earthy and feminist Rigden sisters. The Rigdens advised the baroness that, with the right training, Audrey might have a future in ballet.

When war broke out in September 1939, the baroness brought Audrey home to neutral Holland, where she continued her ballet training at the Arnhem Conservatory of Music in Winja Marova's classes. The German army invaded Holland in May of 1940, and the next five years were spent under the Nazi Occupation. When Audrey was later offered the leading role in the 1959 George Stevens film on the life of Anne Frank, Hepburn turned it down, regarding the story too painfully familiar to her own experience during the war. When she was asked about these experiences, Audrey said, "Interviewers try to bring it up so often, but it's painful to think about. It was a long time ago, and I'm sure other people have been through much worse. I dislike talking about it because I feel it's not something that should be linked to publicity. . . . I wouldn't have missed it for the world—anything that happens to you is valuable. Just the same, mingled in all the nightmares I've had are the war, and the cold clutch of human terror. I've experienced both."

The Germans issued identity cards for people over fifteen years of age. The cards of Jews were stamped with a conspicuous "J." Although her van Heemstra ancestry included some Jewish blood, Audrey and her mother were spared the "J," because it was either too remote or diluted to be noticed by the Reich bureaucracy. Nevertheless, most of their property was seized. The baroness gave up the van Heemstra mansion, which was later used as headquarters by Nazi officers, in exchange for a small flat over a shop in central Arnhem. To prevent the Germans from identifying her as British and therefore an enemy, Audrey was to be known only as Edda van Heemstra, and she was forbidden to speak English.

In 1942, Audrey's uncle, Count Otto van Limburg Stirum, a well-known magistrate in Arnhem, and four other men were executed on August 15, 1942, in reprisal for an act of sabotage by the Dutch Resistance. In the summer of 1943, Audrey's half-brother Ian was rounded up with other local young men and forced into a German labor camp, and her cousin, an adjucant in the royal court, was also slain by the Germans. Audrey recalled her experiences years later:

I saw whole families with children and babies thrown into cattle wagons, trains with big wooden wagons and just a tiny opening on the roof. . . . I remember very sharply one little boy standing with his parents on the platform, very pale, very blond, wearing a coat that was much too big for him, and he stepped onto the train. I was a child observing a child. . . . We saw young men put up against the wall and shot, and they'd close the street and then open it, and you could pass by again. If you read [Anne Frank's] diary, I've marked one place where she says, 'Five hostages shot today.' That was the day my uncle was shot. And in this child's words I was reading about what was inside me and is still there. It was a catharsis for me. This child who was locked up in four walls had written a full report of everything I'd experienced and felt. . . . The things I saw during the occupation made me very realistic about life and I have remained so ever since. . . . I came out of the war grateful to be alive and certain that human relations are the most important thing, much more than wealth, food, luxury, a career and every other thing you can mention.

To aid the Resistance, Audrey danced with her classmates for fund-raising events performed secretly behind black-curtained windows. "We danced to scratchy old recordings of highlights from *Swan Lake, The Nutcracker,* and *Giselle,* which has always been my favorite among the classical ballets." She admitted, "I always had to be the boy in a pas de deux, because I was too tall to play the girl."

Her demure appearance apparently made Audrey a natural courier for the Resistance; she occasionally carried forged ration cards and false identity papers hidden in her shoes, schoolbag, or on her bicycle. On one occasion, she witnessed Nazis herding Jewish families into railroad cars bound for the concentration camps. In September 1944, in part to punish the Dutch for the role of the Resistance in an Allied incursion across the Rhine into Germany, the Nazis razed Arnhem, including the Conservatory of Music. The populace was evacuated on twenty-four hours' notice. Audrey and her mother left on foot, walking five miles to Grandpa van Heemstra's home in Velp, witnessing hundreds collapsing of hunger on the way out of the city. With food scarce during the occupation, Audrey became thin and anemic. This period of malnutrition is reported to have permanently damaged her constitution, and in later years resulted in false rumors of anorexia.

Audrey's more than proverbially sweet sixteenth birthday, May 4, 1945, coincided with the liberation of the Netherlands by Canadian troops. Audrey recalled, "We whooped and hollered and danced for joy. I wanted to kiss every one of them. The incredible relief of being free—it's something that's hard to verbalize." The International Red Cross and the United Nations Relief Agency rallied to the war-ravaged Dutch citizenry with food and medicine. Desperately needed CARE packages also helped Arnhem gradually restore itself.

After the war, Audrey resumed formal study of ballet. As an art and ideal, dance helped sustain her during difficult years, and so it seems natural that the performing arts would take their place alongside humanitarian activity in her life. Audrey never completed the schooling interrupted by the Nazi Occupation of Arnhem.

BRITISH RESIDENCY

1948–1952

and DISCOVERY

THE VAN HEEMSTRA FORTUNES HAD BEEN LOST to the Nazi occupation, and so the baroness secured stable employment managing a flower shop in Amsterdam and a flat nearby for she and sixteen-year-old Audrey to share.

Audrey's talent and passion for dance was palpable, and she was offered city-funded lessons by Sonia Gaskell, a progressive instructor comfortable with the avant-garde as well as jazz interpretation and the classics. The subsidy was cut in 1948, and Gaskell closed her studio and moved to Paris. The baroness considered following, but decided instead to move with her daughter to Britain.

While her mother pursued immigration, Audrey applied for a bit part in a 1948 Dutch industrial film for KLM airlines to help raise cash for the move. Audrey won the role, which was silent and required only that she be pretty, by auditioning in her fanciest evening dress, hat, and long gloves. At the same time, Audrey sought and secured a position in the London dance class of the eminent ballerina Marie Rambert, a former trainer with Les Ballets Russes, who had mentored the dancers Nijinsky and Pavlova in creating a fashion and artistic sensation in the West (epitomized by the riot after the Stravinsky *Rite Of Spring*/Ballet Russes debut in 1913).

After arriving in Britain, Audrey found work with a London modeling agency that regularly availed themselves of Mlle Rambert's pupils for modeling candidates. She also joined her classmates at casting calls for burlesque, vaudeville, and chorus dancers, landing her first role on the professional stage around Christmas of 1948 in an adaptation of the hit Broadway musical *High Button Shoes*. "I was finally earning money as a dancer," Audrey said later of the experience. "Maybe it wasn't the kind of dancing I dreamed of, but I was out of the classroom and into the real world. I loved being in a musical show. For the first time, I felt the pure joy of living."

Bitten by the theater bug, Audrey ended classes with Mlle Rambert and applied to musical revues around town, landing a role in producer Cecil Landau's hit 1949 revue *Sauce Tartare,* which ran for 437 performances at the Cambridge Theatre. She also performed in *Sauce Piquante,* Landau's next revue, which opened in April 1950 very soon after *Sauce Tartare* closed. The two revues kept Audrey busy with theater work, although she continued to do occasional modeling jobs. Cecil sensed Audrey's potential for lead parts, but saw her as professionally rough around the edges. He arranged for character actor Felix Aylmer to mentor her—among other things, refining her British accent and encouraging her to lower the pitch of her speaking voice.

During its run, *Sauce Piquante* was altered and condensed into a revue called *Summer Nights,* which was presented as a floor show at Ciro's Supper Club in London. It was in the cast of this show that Audrey was noticed by casting director Robert Lennard, who recommended her to producer Mario Zampi for a leading role in his comedy *Laughter in Paradise.* Audrey did not win the role, but she was offered a bit part as cigarette-girl in a nightclub scene.

Audrey's first agent found small parts for her in several British pictures in 1951, including *Young Wives' Tale, One Wild Oat,* and *The Lavender Hill Mob* (with but one line spoken to Guy Middleton). In 1952, Audrey graduated to third billing in what was her best-suited and most substantial role to date, a ballet dancer and sister to the female lead in

Thorold Dickinson's *The Secret People,* a story about European political terrorists in the London underground made by Ealing Studios.

The Secret People did not do well commercially; but her next film would prove to be Audrey's last project in relative obscurity. British film production, distribution, and exhibition company Associated British assigned Audrey to a comedy on the French Riviera with each scene to be filmed twice, once in French for the release *Nous irons à Monte Carlo* and again in English for *Monte Carlo Baby.* While filming in Monte Carlo at the Hotel de Paris, Audrey was noticed by the octogenarian French novelist Colette, who, from her wheelchair, aided by her husband Maurice Goudeket, watched the filming at the hotel. Over the next two days, Colette became increasingly sure that in Audrey she had found the perfect actress for the role of Gigi in the upcoming Broadway adaptation of her 1944 novella. Even before being introduced to the actress, Colette cabled her American stage adaptor, Anita Loos: "Don't cast your Gigi until you receive my letter."

Gigi is a story about a canny sixteen-year-old schoolgirl being prepared as a courtesan in her family's tradition who finds unlikely true love with the man for whom she is being groomed as mistress. Colette is reported to have said to her husband, "I have no worries about that one understanding the role of Gigi. She was born understanding all the secrets women use to get their own way."

Audrey naturally seized the opportunity to come to the United States to participate in the production. After previews in Philadelphia, she appeared as Gigi in the show's Broadway premiere, on November 24, 1951. The reviews were generally mixed, but praise for Audrey was nearly unanimous. Her opening night performance, at which Colette was present, generated three solo curtain calls and a standing ovation. *Variety* wrote, "Miss Hepburn has real talent as well as a magnetic personality," and two other papers prophetically called her "the acting find of the year."

PICTURE POST, England, Dec. 15, 1951

NOVELLA, Italy, Jan. 2, 1955

VISTO, Italy, Apr. 10, 1954

OGGI, Italy, Jan. 14, 1954
An unusual early modeling assignment with Audrey depicting the gamine outdoorswoman.

CINÉ REVUE, France, Dec. 14, 1951
Primping for the camera during filming of Monte Carlo Baby, 1951.

CINÉ REVUE

32 PAGES
9 FR.

3e ANNÉE ■ N° 50
1er DECEMBRE 1951

Paraît
tous les vendredis

LA PRODIGIEUSE ASCENSION DE AUDREY HEPBURN,
vedette de « Nous Irons à Monte-Carlo »

NOTRE FILM-ROMAN COMPLET
avec Henri Genès et Philippe Lemaire

★

ELOKUVA AITTA, Finland, Nov. 22, 1952
CINÉ REVUE, France, 1952
*"Nautical dandy" was but one of several modes
explored before Audrey's style-sense had stabilized.*

ABC FILM REVIEW, England, March 1951
Audrey's first appearance as featured "cover girl."
THEATRE ARTS, United States, February 1952
POINT DE VUE, France, Apr. 8, 1954
STRIP, Belgium, Aug. 24, 1963
CIRO'S CLUB, England, 1949
Original 1949 theatrical program for Cecil Landau's revue Sauce Tartare.

EVERYBODY'S, England, Jan. 5, 1952

DANCING TIMES, England, March 1952
Audrey's role in The Secret People *as danseuse by day, political assassin by night, resulted in this crossover publicity in British* Dancing Times *magazine.*

PICTUREGOER, England, May 5, 1951

PICTUREGOER, England, Dec. 13, 1950
This 1950 ensemble shot of Elstree Studios contract players and personnel on the cover of British Picturegoer *is Audrey's first magazine cover appearance.*

ILLUSTRATED, England, Jun. 2, 1951
Audrey's youth is emphasized in this British maga-
zine's portrayal of her as robust dancer and outdoors-
girl. Prior to Roman Holiday, *Audrey was still "the*
other Hepburn."

PRESSBOOK, United States, 1951
Pressbook sent to theater operators with Monte
Carlo Baby *film reels in 1951.*

everybody's

4

**KAVANAGH
—MAN WHO
CHEATS DEATH
—
GOLDEN SECRET
OF THE ANDES
—
£1000 MUST
BE WON
CROSSWORD**

EVERYBODY'S, England, Sept. 26, 1953
An uncharacteristic early modeling pose. Audrey is uncredited.

THE PLAYGOER, United States, Oct. 27, 1952
Theatrical program for Gigi prior to the date upon which the show was contractually suspended to allow Audrey to shoot Roman Holiday in Rome.

WIENER BILDERWOCHE, Austria, Apr. 18, 1953
A fetching publicity shot in costume as Broadway's Gigi.

THE PLAYGOER, United States, 1953
Theatrical program for the West Coast leg of Gigi's tour, recommenced after the completion of Roman Holiday.

TIT-BITS, England, Jul. 15, 1950
Though Audrey never exploited her childhood ordeal for publicity, journalists found the topic made colorful copy.

PARADE, United States, Mar. 9, 1952

MOVIE FAN, United States, September 1954
After Roman Holiday *several articles appeared that sought to paint prim-seeming Audrey's past as that of an ambitious starlet from saucy cabaret.* Sauce Piquante *and* Sauce Tartare *were indeed brazen burlesque shows replete with a female impersonator and Audrey among the leggy chorus line.*

DANCED IN SHADOW OF THE GESTAPO

Before This.. .She Starved

Audrey Hepburn never expected she'd — **jump from Monte Carlo to Broadway**

NEW YORK CITY.

THERE'S AN autographed portrait standing on the mantel of Audrey Hepburn's hotel room here. A picture of the famous French novelist, Colette, it is inscribed, "To Audrey, the treasure I found on a beach."

On Broadway every night that "treasure" cavorts like a frisky puppy in the title role of Colette's play "Gigi." She portrays a young girl being schooled by relatives to become a man's mistress. But he falls in love with her and they marry.

• In the U.S. a new life is unfolding for Audrey. Underneath her gaiety is a serious, mature outlook. It stems from her harsh experiences in the war.

• Audrey lived in Holland during the war and, young as she was, devoted herself to raising money for the Dutch underground.

• "We held secret concerts in private homes," she recalls. "I was just a tall, gawky child wearing costumes my mother made from old curtains. I danced my own versions of classic ballets. The money we made helped saboteurs in their work against the Nazis."

She Went Hungry

AUDREY had to give up dancing and even school towards the war's end. Food was so scarce she was often weak from hunger.

"We had half a loaf of bread and a pound of potatoes a week," says Audrey. "Not enough for a growing girl!"

"The war taught me to appreciate little things," she says. "Now I'm doing what I like and I have a roof over my head. And now I eat what I like."

Born in Brussels, Audrey went to school in England where she won every dancing prize.

It was her dancing skill that got her into dramatics. After the war, she studied ballet in London. To earn tuition, she got a job in the English version of "High Button Shoes." That led to more dance roles, and to movie bits. Then Audrey was chosen for the lead in "Monte Carlo Baby."

EVERY DAY Audrey forgoes morning sleep to get in ballet practice. "With Audrey ballet is as natural as drinking water," says teacher Olga Tarassova.

(Ray Ventura Productions.) On location in Monte Carlo, she was spotted by Colette and promptly offered the role of "Gigi."

"Coming to America was fabulous," sighs Audrey. "On top of that, I got engaged at the same time!"

Audrey's fiance is James Hanson of London. They plan to marry when "Gigi" closes. However, Audrey will continue her career. She is under contract to Associated British Films and to Paramount in Hollywood.

She's a Realist

THE STAGE is something I couldn't possibly give up. I'll try to make things fit my married life," she says. "I'm a realist. I don't fool myself that it will be easy. If you love each other enough, each one makes concessions."

• For a girl with a star on her dressing room door and two movie contracts, Audrey is refreshingly modest.

• "I'm half way between a dancer and an actress," she confides. "I've got a lot to learn."

• Twenty-two year old Audrey knows what she wants for the future: a career and life with the two people she loves most – her husband-to-be and her mother.

• "But life today has to be taken with a grain of salt," says Audrey thoughtfully. "I'm not a fatalist but I realize that a year from now everything may be changed. Anything can happen. That's why I take life as it comes and enjoy it every minute!"

IN "GIGI," Audrey impresses worldly Michael Evans with her innocence.

continued

WHAT IS AUDREY HIDING?

This is the dignified cheesecake for which Audrey posed (in costume from her new Paramount picture, Sabrina) after ads to hypo Roman Holiday's box-office locked her head onto Terry Moore's body.

That's Audrey at the left end of Sauce Piquant's six-girl chorus line,

faking shock at the antics of famous female impersonator Douglas Byng.

"she'll even forget that she was ever a chorus girl."

Subsequent events proved that she would–which is why tongues are wagging from Hollywood to Broadway: is Audrey Hepburn ashamed of her past?

THE current situation is interesting. Whether she knows it or not, Miss Hepburn handles the press with an indifference that is bringing about antagonism. There was first this edict: no interviews during the Ondine rehearsals. That was understandable; Miss Hepburn had only three hours of sleep nightly for three weeks.

But, said her home studio, magazine-assignment interviews would be fulfilled later. Personable press agent William Fields, a man who's done a lot to show Audrey the ropes, made the same promise for the pro-

ducers of the play: interviews would come after the opening.

Only they didn't. Two of America's outstanding magazines gave her more coverage than they'd ever given a young star–including cover portraits. It was enough to turn any young girl's head, and evidently it did. Miss Hepburn banned further interviews and picture sittings for the rest of the run of Ondine, which she–unquestionably–turned into a number-one smash hit singlehandedly.

This was her explanation to a close friend: "In having those two magazines report me, no actress could ask for more. It's like getting an Academy Award in the magazine field. If I were to lend myself to every feature everybody wants, I wouldn't have time to sleep, eat or study."

continued on page 61

And this is the cheesecake for which much plumper, less dignified Audrey posed in the days she seems to have forgotten–when she wore falsies, net stockings, and her dancing was definitely not ballet.

PARADE, United States, Mar. 9, 1952

LOOK, United States, Feb. 12, 1952
Audrey's first major American cover feature was as an up-and-coming Broadway star in Look *magazine.*

PEOPLE TODAY, United States, Jan. 16, 1952

TIT-BITS, England, Oct. 16, 1954
A piece of early publicity cheesecake from The Secret People (1952) *is exploited by British* Tit-Bits *magazine somewhat after the fact. The proportions are not authentically Audrey's.*

SCRAPBOOK
A page from fan-made scrapbook shows Audrey in a playful mood.

MADEMOISELLE, United States, March 1952
Mademoiselle ran this spread featuring items from the wardrobe of Gigi *intended for the pixie "that knew the sex appeal of innocence."*

UNCENSORED, United States, December 1954

ROMAN HOLIDAY

1953

IN SEPTEMBER 1951, BEFORE SHE LEFT LONDON FOR New York to begin rehearsals for *Gigi,* Audrey was among five British actresses screen-tested for the female lead in *Roman Holiday,* a Paramount production that had already secured Gregory Peck as the male lead. By Audrey's good fortune, the tests were conducted for director William Wyler by British director Thorold Dickinson, with whom she had established a relaxed and easy rapport several months prior when he directed *The Secret People* (1952). During her test, Audrey was nervous and tentative, but Dickinson kept the tape rolling after having called "cut." Audrey perked up, kidded with him, and laughed. The extra footage charmed Wyler, and was rumored to be instrumental in his offering Audrey the role.

The screenplay concerns an errant European Princess Ann (country unnamed) who plays hooky from her state duties while visiting Rome. The princess escapes from her bed, and is befriended by a journalist who joins her for the rest of her "holiday." Some innocent romance ensues before the anticlimax, when the princess and journalist say goodbye publicly after reassuming their respective professional roles. Audrey fans seem to agree unanimously that this film and character were a perfect vehicle for the grand debut of the elfin, twenty-three-year-old bit-part player with British diction and a regal bearing cultivated at the ballerina's bar.

The screenplay was written in 1948 by blacklisted Dalton Trumbo, although it was credited in the official release to his "front," Ian McLellan Hunter. The film was released in 1953, and there was certainly pre-publicity benefit from the 1952 revelation that Princess Margaret of England wished to marry a British military captain, but to do so would have to give up her title and place in the line of succession (the captain had been divorced). Also, the topic benefitted from public recollection of the still-recent 1936 abdication of the British throne by Edward VIII, who wished to marry Wallis Simpson, a twice-divorced American.

The alchemy of Audrey's presence in the film, the qualities she embodied in the character—royal but down-to-earth, poised but natural, demure but ambitious—and the way her image was presented surrounding its release made *Roman Holiday* the first of her definitive screen and public appearances. Bill Tusher, in *Motion Picture and Television Magazine,* February 1954, enthused, "Audrey Hepburn is without doubt the most refreshing thing to hit Hollywood in years. The willowy, dark-haired Belgian-born British subject has been likened to Bergman at her most magnificent, a Garbo at her greatest. The French novelist, Colette . . . saw in her another Katharine Hepburn. A leading national magazine backed up this judgment by hailing her as Audrey the 'New Hepburn'. 'When she finds her final place in the firmament,' Colette said long before Audrey turned loose her enchanting powers in *Roman Holiday,* 'there will be two great fixed stars named Hepburn, to the confusion of astronomers, but to the delight of theater-goers.'"

In *Cue Magazine,* July 18, 1953, Audrey's image in the as-yet-to-be released film moved journalist Jesse Zunser to make serious inroads into his thesaurus when announcing the film's premiere the following month: "She is: demure, mischievous, puckish, pert, naive, passionate, captivating, beguiling, hoydenish, disarming, sensitive, alluring, saintlike, coquettish, talented, dedicated, irresistible and ambitious." Trumbo's original story had been first purchased in 1948 for the fledgling Liberty Films Studio owned by Academy Award–winning director Frank Capra, who had intended the project to be filmed in

Italy with Elizabeth Taylor and Cary Grant as the stars. The film came to Paramount when the studio purchased Liberty Films and its assets. Paramount balked at Capra's expensive location and stars, and asked him to make the film in Hollywood. Capra walked out. The option went to director William Wyler, who had been nominated for directorial Academy Awards six times in ten years (winning twice). Wyler's comparative clout allowed him to stipulate filming on location in Rome, but he had to live with the trade-off that Paramount would hold his budget to $1 million (less than they had budgeted for Capra). This meant that the film would be shot in more economical black and white, rather than in color and created the opportunity for an unknown to be cast in the lead.

The wardrobe design for *Roman Holiday* was assigned to eventual eight-time Academy Award–winner Edith Head. A Paramount veteran, Head started as assistant to Howard Greer in 1923, and later assisted his successor, Travis Banton. After Banton left Paramount in 1938, Head was appointed the first female director of a major studio's wardrobe department. Highlights of her career included dressing Clara Bow, Mae West, Gloria Swanson, Veronica Lake, Grace Kelly, Elizabeth Taylor, and Ingrid Bergman. It was Head's habit to work closely with the actresses, and unknown starlet Audrey Hepburn would be no exception. For *Roman Holiday,* which was shot during the very hot Italian summer and fall of 1952, Head worked with Audrey to develop not only the royal formal wear, but also the casual summer styles worn throughout the film. One characteristic ensemble agreed upon was a casual re-interpretation of Dior's "New Look" launched five years earlier: a fitted, white, cotton button-down shirt with rolled up sleeves, tucked into a full, gathered cotton skirt cinched at the waist by a thick belt, with a silk kerchief worn around the neck.

"Trying to make someone like Audrey, who has so much hauteur, look anything but chic is very difficult," wrote Head in *Edith Head's Hollywood.* "I had to adjust the length of the skirt, for instance, making it too long so that she looked somewhat dowdy. I used fabric that was limp to create the impression that she just didn't care what she wore. The costuming was very important in this film—it told the story. First, she was a fairy-tale princess, then she became a sporty, wild, happy, very real person who had no regard for her appearance." Head's practice of serving dramatic purpose first and contemporary style second, when possible, conformed to general studio policy that eschewed emulation of cutting-edge fashion, to avoid having their films seem dated by the time of their release. Head was a favorite with filmmakers for her versatility and efficiency, designing a wide range of superbly engineered and thoughtfully and tastefully considered theatrical clothes. Some more cutting-edge designers, such as Gilbert Adrian at MGM, were favorites of couture-attuned stars, but Head's method was to design more to enhance the drama, and less specifically to enhance the star or play to modern fashion. Although Head never lost sight of the fact that she was designing for movie stars, her approach would eventually lead to tension with Hepburn.

The fashion world felt the impact of *Roman Holiday* not specifically through clothing, but through Audrey's expression of character, an attitude and a will to playful action, such as is displayed when Princess Ann impulsively ducks into a Roman barbershop and has her long hair shorn to a dove-like cloche. Shunning traditional restrictions in clothes and attitude, Audrey/Princess Ann effectively advocated youthful independence and signaled a coming chic. Audrey's low-key, pixie style and character embodied a style shift that would develop over the coming decades.

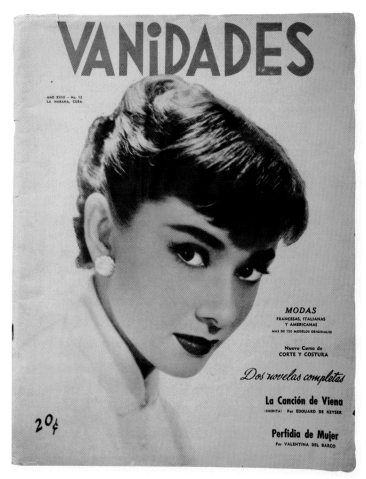

LE SOIR ILLUSTRE, France, Feb. 11, 1954
VANIDADES, Cuba, January 1954
BILLED BLADET, Denmark, Mar. 16, 1954
BILLED BLADET, Denmark, Sept. 29, 1953

BILLED
BLADET

BERØMT
PAA EN NAT

blev den irsk-hollandske
Skuespillerinde Audrey
Hepburn. Født i Belgien,
opvokset i Holland, ud-
dannet i England, blev
hun opdaget af Forfatter-
inden Colette i Monte
Carlo. Aldeles ukendt i
USA fik hun Titelrollen i
»Gigi«, da Stykket skul-
de opføres paa Broad-
way. Da hun vaagnede
op Morgenen efter Pre-
mieren, var hun berømt.
Hurtigt meldte Holly-
wood sig, og Audrey fik
Hovedrollen i »Roman
Holiday«. Hendes Præ-
station var Sensationen

O CRUZIERO, Brazil, March 1956
Brazilian Cruziero *magazine ran these still captures from the now-famous screen test through which pre-fame Audrey won the role of Princess Ann in* Roman Holiday.

APU, Finland, Oct. 4, 1954

ME NAISET, Finland, October 1954

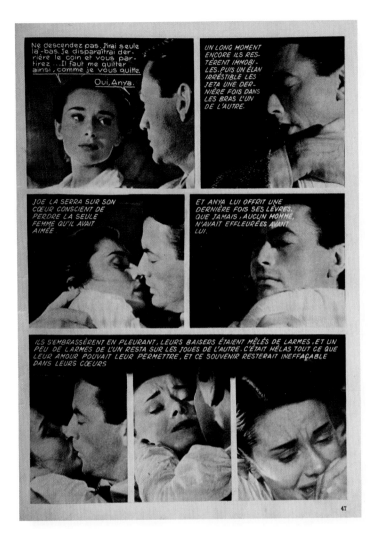

PHOTO ROMAN, France, Feb. 12, 1958
French Photo Roman *applied the graphic novel treatment to the entirety of the* Roman Holiday *film.*

FESTIVAL, Italy, Aug. 29, 1953
Incredibly, the 3-D glasses are still attached inside, but, unfortunately, the 3-D images are not of Audrey.

FRANKFURTER ILLUSTRIERTE, Germany, Oct. 16, 1954

EVERYBODY'S, Israel, October 1953

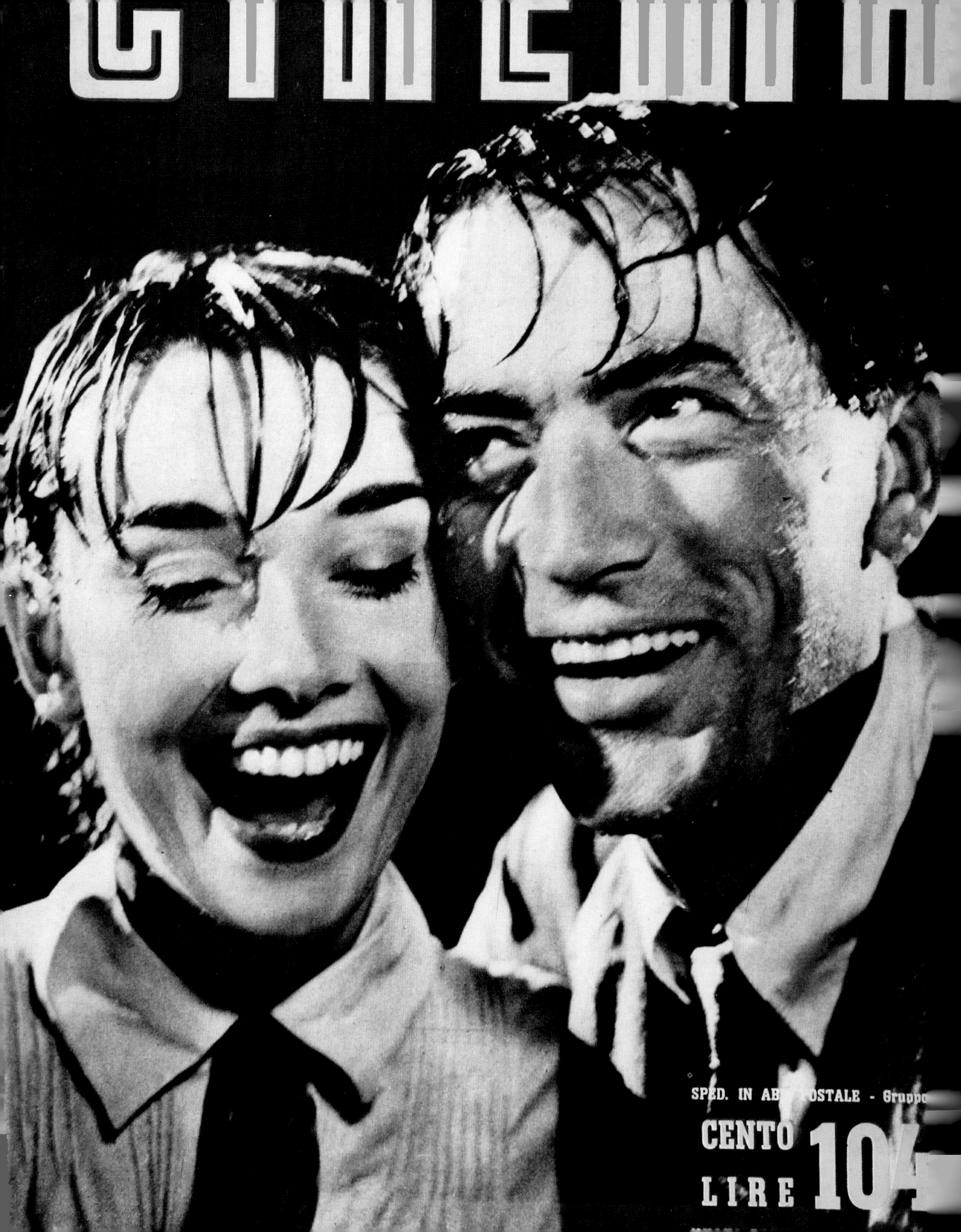
SPED. IN AB OSTALE - Gruppo
CENTO
LIRE
104

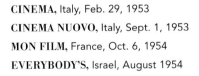

CINEMA, Italy, Feb. 29, 1953
CINEMA NUOVO, Italy, Sept. 1, 1953
MON FILM, France, Oct. 6, 1954
EVERYBODY'S, Israel, August 1954

EIGA NO TOMO, Japan, May 1954

MUNDO URUGUAYO, Uruguay, Jun. 17, 1954

Audrey's early gamine image presaged a movement toward an exuberant youth culture in the 1950s. Prior to this time, aspiring youth generally sought to emulate the affectations of "adult" vogue.

SCREEN PICTORIAL, Japan, Summer 1954

THE MOVIES, Thailand, 1954

PICTURE SHOW, England, Oct. 3, 1953

PICTUREGOER October 11 1952

The Future belongs to AUDREY

"Roman Holiday"
...pburn as the tops

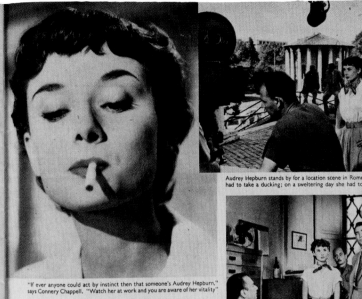

"If ever anyone could act by instinct then that someone's Audrey Hepburn," says Connery Chappell. "Watch her at work and you are aware of her vitality"

Audrey Hepburn stands by for a location scene in Rome. One cold night she had to take a ducking; on a sweltering day she had to wear a lined nightie

Despite their expertness, Audrey Hepburn and Gregory Peck, co-stars of Roman Holiday, have had to re-act scenes as many as twenty times or more

... way is every bit as expert, will tell you the same thing.

Of course, Audrey Hepburn is a lucky girl. She is extremely young, her experience is very limited, and it is given to few people to play lead with Peck in a film by Wyler.

But as you watch her at work, snapping into a scene, her intense and instinctive vitality is there to be seen at once; the challenging flash of the eye occurs at precisely the right ...

... heights, and disliking staircases that spin around a hollow well, I found it no place for a visitor.

But Audrey, who lived there through the summer with her mother, found it a perfect change from the noisy bustle of the Rome streets, fussy with the fretful hooters of hundreds of motor scooters, and from the ex...

... was necessary for Audrey to work on a one-room set at the Cinecittà Studios on one of the hottest days of the year. The temperature varied between 120 and 130, and the young star was wearing a long wig and a flannel nightdress, which had been heavily lined in order that it would hang better for photo...

PICTUREGOER, England, Oct. 11, 1952
England was the first to recognize (too late) that Audrey would become a great star while her first Hollywood film, Roman Holiday, *was still only in production.*

RIVISTA DEL CINEMATOGRAFO, Italy, April 1954

NOVELA FILME, Portugal, 1953

SABRINA

1954– 1955

ANYONE WHO HAD SEEN THE RUSHES FOR *Roman Holiday* before the film's release in 1953 could see that newcomer Audrey Hepburn would become very hot property for Paramount Studios. Audrey was under contract to them for just two more films, so Paramount weighed her next vehicle carefully. In 1953, director Billy Wilder secured for Paramount the rights to a current Broadway success called *Sabrina Fair*, which he believed to be ideal for Audrey Hepburn. It was the story of the forlorn daughter of a Long Island chauffeur who returns from finishing school in France and captures the hearts of both sons of her father's wealthy employer. While *Roman Holiday* had cast her in an inspirational reverse-Cinderella fairy tale, the next vehicle, a straightforward Cinderella story, would deviate only slightly from *Holiday*'s success formula.

Adapted for the screen by the original playwright, Samuel Taylor, with Audrey in mind, the film would be called simply *Sabrina*. With the casting of William Holden (thirty-six years old) and Humphrey Bogart (fifty-five years old) as her leading men, a tradition was established of significantly, often distractingly, older leading men playing opposite Audrey, who at the time of *Sabrina*'s filming was twenty-three.

Just as filming for *Sabrina* was about to begin, *Roman Holiday* premiered to sensational notices at New York's Radio City Music Hall on August 27, 1953. (Audrey would win an Oscar for Best Actress for the film the following year.) Suddenly an authentic overnight sensation, Audrey was now able to demand contractual concessions. Although Edith Head had been assigned as wardrobe designer for *Sabrina*, Audrey's first imperial dictum as a "star" was that she herself be permitted to handpick a couture designer to create costumes for the portion of the film that portrayed Sabrina after her return from finishing school in France. Billy Wilder backed the idea, and so Audrey was sent to Paris to meet with her first choice, the legendary Cristobal Balenciaga.

Balenciaga, who was born in San Sebastian in 1895, was hailed as Spain's leading couturier by the early 1930s, and he had moved to Paris in 1936. An innovative and daring designer, Balenciaga was also a purist who, after having witnessed the American ready-to-wear industrial machine of the 1940s, vowed never to employ mechanical manufacture for his creations. By doing so, he gave up international enterprise, but garnered the highest admiration of fellow couturiers (André Courrèges, Emanuel Ungaro, Hubert de Givenchy, and Christian Dior) and those who followed high fashion. In 1939, he had introduced a dropped shoulder line with a cinched waist and full hips, a style that foreshadowed Dior's influential "New Look" of 1947; he was the first to subsequently deviate from Dior's influence with a movement toward suits in the early '50s; and he would introduce the "sack dress," collarless blouse, and other innovations later in the '50s. Photographer Cecil Beaton said of him, "Balenciaga has founded the future of Fashion." It's clear why Audrey would have been keen to work with him.

Arriving in late summer, Audrey found that Balenciaga was unavailable because of the traditional seasonal rush in preparation for the fall collections. Audrey suggested to Paramount that they try to make arrangements with another young designer, Hubert de Givenchy, a talented Balenciaga protégé and former apprentice to Elsa Schiaparelli, who had opened his own house in Paris just two years earlier. Despite the fact that Givenchy had already drawn rave reviews for his first collections, Audrey hoped that he wasn't so established that he wouldn't appreciate the opportunity to design for Hollywood even in the seasonal rush.

Givenchy agreed to receive an actress that Paramount identified only as "Miss Hepburn," by which he assumed it would be veteran film great Katharine Hepburn. He was admittedly surprised and, at first, disappointed when doe-eyed Audrey entered his studio. They would go on to enjoy a celebrated, lifelong collaboration, but at this point, as delighted as Givenchy was to meet Audrey Hepburn, the pressures of the season kept his design focus on his collection. He suggested that Audrey choose from the pieces from a prior collection still on hand, and offered her sketches and samples to aid in the fabrication of his designs back at Paramount Studios. Audrey chose two finished outfits for *Sabrina*, and with the Givenchy sketchbook and samples in hand, flew back to the United States.

The ensembles are now legendary. The first was the chic "Glen Cove Suit" of Oxford-gray wool with a cinched waist, double-breasted, scoop-neck jacket, and slim, calf-length, vented skirt and pale gray turban and white gloves in which Sabrina arrives at the train station upon her return from Paris, accessorized for the inadvertent seduction of David Larrabee with faintly bohemian drop-hoop earrings. Second was the adapted-for-Audrey "Inez de Castro" strapless, white organdy ball gown with floral embroidery in black silk thread and jet beads with a detachable train, in which Sabrina creates a sensation at the Larrabee's Long Island house party.

And third was the black cotton, ribbed-piqué cocktail dress, with collarbone-concealing, soon to be influential, décolleté bateau neckline, deeply cut "V" in back, with strap ties forming a perky bow at each shoulder. Audrey had separately selected a black lace rhinestone-flecked chapeau from Givenchy's warehouse, and the outfit was finished in the film by quarter-length, black satin gloves. This third outfit is the one in which Sabrina arrives for her second date with Linus at the Larrabee Building.

Edith Head did design some of Audrey's wardrobe for the film, but according to Paddy Calistro, co-author of Head's 1983 posthumous memoir *Edith Head's Hollywood,* she was disappointed when Audrey walked into their initial costume meeting for *Sabrina* "armed with a wardrobe designed by Hubert de Givenchy, the noted couturier, who had also provided her with a notebook of suggested sketches." Calistro continues, "When Edith presented her sketches to the actress, instead of the quiet, accepting young thing who had greeted her the year before (during costume meetings for *Roman Holiday*), an assertive Audrey Hepburn pulled out the sketch pad and samples to show Edith exactly what she wanted."

The item of most controversy was the black, boatneck cocktail dress, which many clothing manufacturers copied and dubbed Décolleté Sabrina, or "the Sabrina neckline." The design for this dress had been created by Givenchy and was contained in the notebook that Audrey brought back with her from France. According to Calistro, after Head's death in 1981, wardrobe department coworkers at Paramount confided that although Head had always claimed the dress as her original design, it was not in fact hers. She had merely supervised its manufacture at Paramount from Givenchy's sketch. Head purchased the dress from Paramount, and added it to a small costume collection that she eventually presented as a retrospective of her own designs to show all over the world. It remains unclear why such a gifted, accomplished, and lauded designer would claim parentage of a particular garment she did not design. It might be that she felt her direction and oversight in the manufacture qualified as creative authorship. Or, it might suggest embarrassment or humiliation at having her sketchbook of faux French couture designs set aside by Audrey in favor of "the real thing" by Givenchy.

Among the outfits Head did design for the movie were Sabrina's canoeing outfit—the Montauk Yacht Club—inspired ensemble of white deck shorts and an oversized button-down madras blouse wrapped twice around Audrey's twenty-inch waist. Head also designed a wonderfully dowdy, pleated, grayish-brown pinafore for the scenes in which Audrey helps her father wash the Larrabee Rolls Royce, perches in a tree ogling the Larrabee's society dance, and finally attempts suicide by carbon monoxide poisoning in the Larrabee garage. The structure of the film itself caused Givenchy's couture to outshine the portion of the wardrobe Head had created. Head declined to share credit on the film with Givenchy, and did not mention his contribution when she received an Oscar for its costume design (one of six nominations for the film, including best actress for Audrey, which she did not win). In a sense, because Audrey chose the Givenchy fashions essentially off the rack, and the French designer did not make anything expressly for the film, it could be said that Givenchy deserves no more credit for Sabrina's wardrobe

design than Levi-Strauss and Hanes deserve for James Dean's wardrobe on *Rebel Without a Cause*. But in that case, it could be argued that for her taste and selection, Audrey would be deserving of co-credit with Head.

Though there were occasional dissenters, such as critic Clayton Cole, who wrote in British *Films & Filming*, "Surely the vogue for asexuality can go no further than this weird hybrid with butchered hair," the style and couture in *Sabrina* introduced a new direction in feminine glamorization. Audrey's outfits played down the then-fashionable and idolized female bosom and hips, and instead emphasized grace of movement. Though at this point Givenchy and Hepburn had not established a true collaboration, their points of accord were clear: a refined elegance and unassuming simplicity—Audrey's easy flexibility in switching whimsically between boyishness and modest femininity; Givenchy's quiet defiance of affectation and elitism, demonstrated in his first collection being created entirely of economical gingham. Other influential elements of fashion flowing from *Sabrina* include the embroidered slipper-flats created by Salvatore Ferragamo, the "shoemaker to the stars" whom Audrey had met while making *Roman Holiday*. Ferragamo's style evolved from purely exotic designs to an embracing of combined style and comfort as he studied metatarsal anatomy at the University of Southern California before leaving the United States in 1927.

Two hairstyles sported by Audrey in *Sabrina* were influential throughout the '50s: the short-bangs ponytail utilized in the first half of the film, and the neatly trimmed, shorter, dove-like style seen after Sabrina's transformation. The bangs cut furthered and refined the style sported by the likes of pinup icon Bettie Page, and persisted decades later in retro-swing and gothic subcultures. The short cut was not a fashion innovation. It followed the vogue for short cuts in the '20s and Ingrid Bergman's tousled pageboy Joan of Arc cut in 1948. But again, Audrey's stylish refinement brought the cut to more high-fashion taste. It is interesting to note that a trendier resetting of the Joan of Arc cut, filtered through the Audrey style, premiered in Otto Preminger's 1957 production *Saint Joan*, featuring Jean Seberg. Preminger had originally offered the part to Audrey, but there was no place for her then-husband Mel Ferrer in the production, so Audrey turned it down—and so the role and the haircut went to Seberg. Preminger's subsequent film, *Bonjour Tristesse,* again starring Seberg, further popularized the style, with the same coif now christened the "Cecile Cut," after Seberg's character.

As early as 1950, *Vogue's* "Young As You Are" campaign premiered a series of articles encouraging young readers to celebrate their youth through independent style. *Vogue* mandated that fashion priorities of the recent past, including its own emphasis upon sophistication and class mobility, should be viewed "with amused tolerance." One example of a new youth style that emerged on its own terms was the age-and-class-indifferent beatnik/bohemian mode originating in St-Germain-des-Prés in Paris. Audrey, its mainstream ambassador during the early phase of her career, eventually evolved into haute couture, and in doing so, passed the mantle of bohemian celebrity style to Brigitte Bardot.

In a November 1954 article for *Vogue*, Cecil Beaton presented Audrey as a "miracle girl" who transformed the concept of beauty. "Nobody ever looked like her before World War II; it is doubtful that anybody ever did," he continued, "yet we recognize the rightness of this appearance . . . and the proof is that thousands of imitations have appeared." Beaton added that she had "natural grace . . . inner elegance . . . [and an] incandescent glow" and was a "rare phenomenon" and "the public embodiment of our new feminine ideal."

Audrey represented a new style, a departure from conventional celebrity entitlement. She endorsed a casual but sensible ready-to-wear and fuss-free couture and a reliance upon free expression of character and personal sensibility. The message was that women no longer needed to aspire to be "sophisticated" in the older, more matronly style.

ETOKUVA-AITTA, Finland, 1954

IMAGES, Egypt, May 15, 1954

CINÉ REVUE, France, Apr. 9, 1954
The famous black and white Givenchy ball gown from Sabrina.

LIBERTY, Canada, March 1958

BILLED BLADET, Aug. 17, 1954

BILLED BLADET

AUDREY HEPBURN

CINE AVENTURAS, Argentina, May 26, 1955

THIS WORLD, Israel, 1954
On this remarkably surreal 1954 cover of Israeli This World *magazine, Audrey charms in the chapeau she handpicked at Givenchy's studio during her trip there in the late summer of 1953.*

BILD JOURNALEN, Denmark, 1954

ECRAN, Chile, Mar. 29, 1955

PROGRAM, Japan, Sept. 1, 1954

BILD JOURNALEN, Denmark, Jan. 16, 1959

KUVA-POSTI, Finland, May 1955

WERELD-KRONIEK

De W.K. belicht de achtergronden van het drama der

Joodse pleegkinderen

Eigen reportage uit de kloosters van St. Truiden, Banneux en Valmeer !

◆

In dit nummer begint het boeiende levensverhaal van

Audrey Hepburn

met tal van onbekende foto's !

◆

Uitvoerige bijzonderheden over het geruchtmakende

Sensatie proces Montesi

◆

Het geheim van het flatgebouw

een der meest sensationele gebeurtenissen uit de archieven van Scotland Yard !

WERELD-KRONIEK, Netherlands, Mar. 27, 1954

DAMERNAS VÄRLD, Sweden, Apr. 27, 1955

CINE ROMANCE, Portugal, 1954

FILM NEUES PROGRAMM, Germany, May 1954

ILLUSTRIERTER FILM-KURIER, Germany, December 1954

ESTÚDIO REVISTA DE CINEMA, Portugal, Oct. 20, 1954

THE MOVIES, Thailand, 1954

WORLD MOVIES, China, 1954

MARGRIET, Belgium, Oct. 23, 1954

ECRAN, Chile, Mar. 5, 1956

ASAHI CAMERA, Japan, November 1956
REVUE, Germany, Jun. 7, 1958
CAHIERS DU CINEMA, France, December 1954
ÅRET RUNT, Sweden, Apr. 7, 1955
CINE AVENTURAS, Argentina, Jul. 7, 1955

SABRINA, Netherlands, 1954
Top and bottom left: Dutch theatrical program for Sabrina including a sphynx-like pose for its gatefold pinup.

PICTURE SHOW, England, Oct. 23, 1954
Above and facing page: The original play was called Sabrina Fair, and though Billy Wilder shortened the American name for his film to Sabrina, British prints and publicity continued to carry the original play's title.

Sabrina Fair

The fabulously wealthy Larrabee family in their Long Island house. The family consists of Oliver and his wife Maude and their two sons, Linus and David. Linus is the business man of the family, David a happy-go-lucky young man unmindful of the love of Sabrina, the family chauffeur's daughter **Humphrey Bogart** (Linus), **Walter Hampden** (Oliver Larrabee), **Nella Walker** (Maude), **William Holden** (David)

It is Linus who comes to Sabrina's rescue when, because of David, she tries to commit suicide. Her father sends her to Paris to learn cookery **Audrey Hepburn** (Sabrina), **Humphrey Bogart** (Left) At the Parisian school, Sabrina comes under the influence of Baron Saint Fontanelle. He makes her a sophisticated young lady **Marcel Hillaire** (Professor), **Marcel Dalio** (Baron), **Audrey Hepburn**

Two years later, Sabrina returns and is offered a lift from the station by David. Later he realises her identity (Right) To make sure that David marries Elizabeth, the girl chosen to increase the family fortune, Linus sets out to win Sabrina's heart and loses his own (Below) Sabrina realises the situation and is returning to France. David goads Linus into making a desperate dash for the ship **Ellen Corby** (Miss McCardle)

Sabrina is welcomed by her father, who later becomes worried when David and Sabrina spend a great deal of time together. **Audrey Hepburn**, **John Williams** (Thomas Fairchild) And David gaily informs Elizabeth that he will marry her **Ellen Corby**, **Martha Hyer** (Elizabeth), **Francis X. Bushman** (Mr. Tyson), **William Holden**, **Walter Hampden**

CONSTANZE, Germany, March 1957

CINÉ REVUE, France, Apr. 9, 1954
Early publicity for Audrey such as this French magazine spread, emphasized the glamour and style of youth.

WESTERN POINT, China, 1954

SCREEN, Japan, November 1954

STAR STORY, Japan, September 1954

PARTICIPEZ A NOTRE
GRAND CONCOURS
POUR TOUS LES AGES

AUDREY HEPBURN
La princesse charmante de " Vacances Romaines ",
Oscar 1954, reparaît aujourd'hui avec " Sabrina " dans
le rôle d'une jeune Américaine aimant Paris (p. 32-35).

N°14 10 au 17 Février 1955
Afr. du Nord 60f. Maroc 65f.
10 f. belges. 90 cent. suisses 50f

JOURS DE FRANCE, France, Feb. 17, 1955

PHOTO ROMAN, France, Mar. 1, 1957
Sequence from French Photo Roman *magazine
affording several angles of the influential boatneck
dress whose provenance had for decades been a point
of contention in the fashion world. After Edith Head's
death, her assistant finally conceded that she had
fabricated the costume at Paramount studios from a
sketch originally supplied by Givenchy.*

Has Stardom Changed Audrey?

An evening alone with music is Audrey's idea of fun.

She admits heating milk is about extent of her cooking.

They're Whispering That the Hepburn Gal Has Gone High-Hat, That Stage and Screen Successes Have Robbed Her of Humility. Here Is the Record. We'll Leave It to You, the Reader, to Decide If the Rumors Are True or False.

● When she first landed on these shores a couple of years ago, Audrey Hepburn was a complete unknown. But with her overnight success in the Broadway production of *Gigi*, little Audrey was hailed as the greatest acting find in years. Her elfin face, graceful figure and intriguingly accented English, as well as her very obvious dramatic ability scored a knockout over the critics. She became their darling, and Audrey was grateful—so much so that she willingly posed for publicity photos and granted interviews to all comers. With her movie success in *Roman Holiday* and the Academy Award that followed, Audrey became nationally famous. By the time she'd annexed the Antoinette Perry award for the excellence of her stage work in *Ondine*, Missy Hepburn was the most sought-after actress in the world. But as her fame grew, she became more and more difficult to work with. She began to demand star privileges, failed to keep appointments, even refused to sign autographs. And cardinal sin of all, Audrey turned down interviews. An unfortunate incident, which, it seems, was all a misunderstanding, garnered her bad press with a newsman. When he requested an interview, she sent word that while she did not care to talk for publication, she would be pleased to shake his hand if he came backstage. The writer blew his top. However, it seems that in Audrey's native Holland, to shake hands with someone is considered a great honor—and this is what she thought she was doing. Her somewhat queenly attitude prevailed all through the filming of *Sabrina*, Audrey's delightful new Paramount comedy. True, she was cooperative during the actual shooting, but after the day's work was over, she retreated to her apartment, declining all invitations and often spending whole weekends at home alone. Her excuse was that she needed the time to refuel for the next week's work. Last spring, during her Broadway stint in *Ondine*, Audrey went so far as to cut herself off from her own press agent for a short time. When not on stage, she could be reached only by her mother or her co-star and constant companion, Mel Ferrer. Once again, she claimed that she was physically exhausted and that her doctor had warned her against any activity not directly connected with her job. The lovely lass certainly looks frail and delicate, but the fact remains that publicity and interviews are actually a vital part of Audrey's job and if, because of ill health, she cannot spend a lot of time with writers and photographers, then it's to her advantage to be a little more diplomatic when turning down requests. Right now, Audrey's taking a needed rest in Italy. We hope when she returns to America, she will be as charming in person as in reel life.

12 DECEMBER, 1954

MOVIE SECRETS, United States, Dec. 12, 1954
Early on, Audrey's frailness caused her to limit her exposure to journalists and photographers; some spurned reporters were quick to interpret this as an emerging arrogance.

NOVELLA, Italy, Apr. 10, 1955
Audrey's informal and youthful gamine image was a new twist for glamour in 1954.

DŽEPNI MAGAZIN, Poland, 1956
After the rise of her stardom, Audrey managed to charm both genders without trading directly on sex appeal.

LOOK, United States, Mar. 23, 1954

ROTO, United States, Sept. 17, 1955

VECKO JOURNALEN, Sweden, Nov. 13, 1954

CINEMA NUOVO, Italy, Jan. 25, 1955

VECKO-TIDNINGEN SÅNINGSMANNEN, May 15, 1954

FARBIGE ROMANE, Germany, 1955

HOLLYWOOD ROMANCES, United States, 1954
*One of many gossip magazines at the time questioning Mel
Ferrer's motives in courting Audrey.*

EIGA NO TOMO, Japan, May 1954

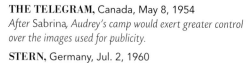

THE TELEGRAM, Canada, May 8, 1954
After Sabrina, Audrey's camp would exert greater control over the images used for publicity.

STERN, Germany, Jul. 2, 1960

FESTIVAL, France, March 1955

LIFE, United States, Dec. 7, 1953
Attempting to demystify her revolutionary appeal in the early days of her Hollywood success, several magazines ran articles by drawing-room psychologists, as here, speculating on "What makes Audrey charm."

LIFE EN ESPAÑOL, United States, Apr. 26, 1954

CINÉ REVUE, France, Jan. 28, 1955
Edith Head yeoman's ensemble for Sabrina's sailing date with Linus Larrabee.

AUDREY HEPBURN

Her producer says: "She is the great star you meet once or twice in a lifetime." Her hairdresser says: "She's the only actress who doesn't gab, read, knit, wriggle, pick her teeth, or eat, while under a drier"

BY MARTIN ABRAMSON PHOTOGRAPHS BY PHILIPPE HALSMAN

In November, 1951, a Broadway publicist named Arthur Cantor sent a message to the New York newspapers and press services which he whimsically marked: "Urgent." "New British actress named Hepburn arriving this morning at Pier 90 to appear in Broadway play. She is a great find. Suggest you send reporters and photographers." Without benefit of telepathy, every editor who received the communique impaled it on a spike reserved for useless trivia, and Miss Hepburn arrived in New York harbor to be greeted by a crashing yawn. The anxious Mr. Cantor scurried around the dock, found one ship-news reporter with time on his hands, and begged him to ask the new arrival a few questions. "Nah," the reporter told him. "I'd rather go have a cup of coffee."

Since that bleak morning in New York, the lives and times of Audrey Hepburn—who happens to be English only in part, with a liberal mixture of Dutch, Irish, French, and Hungarian thrown in as well—have taken several acrobatic twists. First of all there was her pole vault out of her void of total disinterest into a success all sheen and opulence. On the basis of only two stage plays, "Gigi" and "Ondine," and two films, "Roman Holiday" and "Sabrina," she created more of a ruckus in show business than any performer since Bergman, carted off enough trophies—including the coveted Oscar—to fill a Sears-Roebuck warehouse, and mortified the fiercely proud Katharine Hepburn into the discovery that people were calling her "that other Hepburn."

Then with all kinds of golden geese waiting to be plucked in the wake of this hulaballoo, little Audrey suddenly fled the glory trail. She tuned out the blandishments of agents and promoters, the hoarse shouts of movie studios and TV networks, and transferred to a pastoral idyll in Europe, in company with actor Mel Ferrer, whom she married almost over the prostrate bodies of kin, friends, and advisers. Now after more than a year in Garbolike rustication, she has again confounded the know-alls who have been announcing her permanent retirement by popping up as star of what the advertising writers call a "big, Big, BIG picture": the five-million-dollar Paramount epic, "War and Peace."

A Cryptogrammic Success Story

This Cinderella career story, complete with O. Henry deviations, sounds like fantasy—as does Audrey Hepburn's personal story, which ranges from baronial splendor to terror and hunger suffered under the Nazi yoke, then back again to easy street—but the facts are all there and the puzzler is how to explain them. To begin with, the magic of the Hepburn appeal and popularity seems to be based on some kind of sleight-of-hand. Newcomers in show business usually attract attention by their gregariousness, their flair for publicity, and their daring sexual appeal; but Audrey lacks all of these qualities. Furthermore, when she is stripped down feature by feature, she falls dismally short of the accepted standard for movie queens. Her figure is arrow-thin, her eyes are oversized saucers, her hair is close-shorn like a gamin's, her nose is too long, her mouth too wide, her eyebrows dart off strangely like birds in flight, and her front teeth are crooked. "I have often thought of myself as quite ugly," she tells you frankly. "In fact, I used to have quite a complex about it."

Inner complexes aside, however, there is such intoxicating charm in Audrey Hepburn that anyone who sees her forgets the imperfect parts and remembers only that they somehow come out a rapturous whole. It may be elusive fascination but it is irresistible to those exposed to it. Theater audiences who had never heard of Audrey burst into instinctive applause when she first came on stage in "Gigi," and a movie audience in Los Angeles, did precisely the same thing at a sneak preview of "Roman Holiday."

It is powerful enough to eclipse fellow performers, which explains why she was able to steal "Roman Holiday" from such an established star as Gregory Peck, and "Sabrina" from the likes of Humphrey Bogart and William Holden. It also mesmerizes elevator boys and chambermaids who fall over one another to do special things for her, movie cameramen who refer to her as a "living doll," and show *(continued)*

"I believe in setting a goal, and letting nothing divert me from reaching it."

26

Audrey Hepburn, Many-sided Charmer

PHOTOGRAPHS BY MARK SHAW

CONTINUED ON NEXT PAGE 127

AUDREY HEPBURN

FOR HER NEW MOVIE, Paramount's *Sabrina Fair*, Audrey stands ready in make-up and costume to play the title role. Acting the daughter of a chauffeur for a Long Island family, she is courted alternately by her rich employer's two sons.

130

COSMOPOLITAN, United States, October 1955
Audrey flying high for a Cosmo photo shoot.

LIFE, United States, Dec. 7, 1953
Two individul pages from the issue. With only her first hit (Roman Holiday) recently premiered and her second U.S. film (Sabrina) in production, Life magazine, to its credit, unflinchingly trumpets the arrival of a great new star with a remarkably lavish nine-page spread.

EXTRA HORA XXV, Spain, June 1965

CINE MUNDO, Spain, Sept. 17, 1955
The only original design fabricated by Edith Head for Audrey in Sabrina. Audrey's other casual-wear for the film was assembled by Edith from manufactured ready-to-wear elements, while all the formal and chic-wear for Audrey was designed by Hubert de Givenchy.

WIENER FILM REVUE, Austria, April 1955

RADIO CINEMA TÉLÉVISION, France, Feb. 6, 1955

ONDINE, 1954

MARRIAGE *and* ACADEMY AWARD

AUDREY HAD TAKEN LEAVE FROM *GIGI* TO FILM *Roman Holiday,* and she rejoined the cast after filming was complete. After *Gigi* closed in mid-April 1953 in San Francisco, Audrey flew back to London for a reunion with her mother and a well-earned vacation. With the cooperation of Gregory Peck, who was already in Europe shooting *Night People,* Paramount arranged to welcome Audrey with a cocktail bash that would reunite the two stars of the as-yet-to-be released *Roman Holiday.* By several accounts, it was at this party on May 31, 1953, at her costar's flat on Grosvenor Square in London that Audrey first met Gregory Peck's friend Mel Ferrer.

Ferrer was a married but separated American with children, and was then shooting MGM's *Knights of the Round Table* in England. Reportedly, Ferrer was reserved at the party, but Peck encouraged a follow-up and offered Audrey's number to him. (By another, more likely account, Mel had actually missed the party and called Audrey at Peck's encouragement—Audrey had been looking foward to meeting him.) In any case, Audrey had admired Mel's work in *Lili* and told him so during their initial phone conversation in which the two discussed theater at length. It was also tossed about that they might work together in a future play; and according to Ferrer, Audrey asked him to send her a likely script if he found one.

Roman Holiday finally premiered in New York four months later, in August 1953; two months after that, shooting on *Sabrina* was completed. In the lull afterward, Ferrer presented Audrey with a stage vehicle in which he thought they could star together. The play, which had languished unproduced since 1939, was Jean Giraudoux's *Ondine,* a story based on the German legend of a medieval knight and a water nymph. The production opened in New York on February 18, 1954, ran for 157 sold-out performances, and closed on June 26. On March 29, Audrey was awarded Broadway's Antoinette Perry (Tony) Award for her performance as the water nymph. Earlier that same week, she had received an Oscar for her performance in *Roman Holiday.* It was at this time that Hepburn and Ferrer became romantically involved, at first reportedly living together in Audrey's Greenwich Village apartment, and later moving to Jose Ferrer (no relation) and Rosemary Clooney's weekend house at New York's Pound Ridge. Upon learning of the liaison, Mel Ferrer's estranged wife Frances, mother of two of his four children, asked for a divorce, which was hastily completed in Mexico.

Before *Ondine* closed in June, with ink still wet on Ferrer's divorce papers, Hepburn and Ferrer announced engagement plans. They were married on September 24, 1954, in Bürgenstock, Switzerland, and spent a month-long honeymoon at Albano, twenty miles southeast of Rome. At the wedding, Audrey wore a simple, short, Pierre Balmain organdy dress with a rounded neckline and white gloves, and her head was crowned with a chaplet of white roses.

It was said that Ferrer had assumed a paternalistic attitude toward Audrey during the production of *Ondine,* to the extent of undermining the director, Alfred Lunt, and there was speculation that Ferrer now played a svengali role in the actress's life. This reputation dogged their entire married lives (they would divorce in 1968), and was furthered by the relative commercial and artistic failures of the 1959 Ferrer-directed *Green Mansions,* in which Audrey starred.

Mel told journalist Lloyd Shearer in *Parade*, August 21, 1955:

I know that I've been accused of being Audrey's Svengali. But people just don't realize how many interviews one little statue like the Academy Award calls for. As Audrey's husband, I have a responsibility to look after her health. We try to do as much as we can, but it's impossible to satisfy everyone. A year or so ago, when we were doing Ondine, *we were invited to a circus charity at Madison Square Garden. Had to wear costumes, ride horses, the whole routine. It was for a good cause, so we said yes. As soon as the curtain lowered on our own show, we changed clothes, rushed like mad to get over to the Garden. Audrey, believe me, was on the verge of fainting. All the photographers gathered around, started shooting. I looked at Audrey. She was growing whiter by the second. "Hold it up, fellows," I begged, "just for a minute. Isn't there some place Audrey can sit down and catch her breath? She's going to pass out." The photographer got insulted. They accused me of being high-handed. They didn't know that Audrey's doctor had forbidden her to work, warned her about an impending collapse, told her to get away for a long vacation or he wouldn't be responsible. They were just sore because they didn't get a picture.*

Deserved or not, Ferrer certainly would have invited resentment in commercial Hollywood circles for his dedication to the cutting edge (and unprofitable) La Jolla Playhouse, which he co-founded with Gregory Peck and Dorothy McGuire in 1947, while remaining eager to fill both the actor's and director's chairs back in the commercial end of the business. This dichotomy could have been seen as not only ironic, but presumptuous. Nevertheless, his idealistic and sincere commitment to the craft of acting had been the topic of his first conversation with Audrey, and provided the basis for their long partnership.

As for who directed whom in *Ondine,* Audrey said at the time "Mr. Ferrer is only trying to be helpful, and I think it is horrid the way some reporters write about it. I appreciate the way he guides me." She later said of Ferrer in the celebrity gossip magazine *Exposed* (August 1956): "He had such definite tastes and opinions on books, plays, people, politics. Compared to him, all the pleasant fellows I had known in the past had been intellectual dwarves."

74

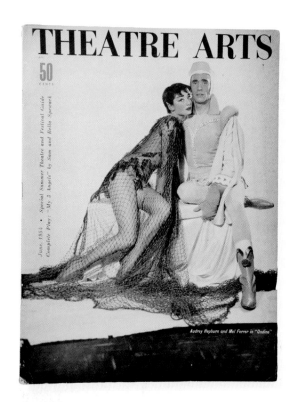

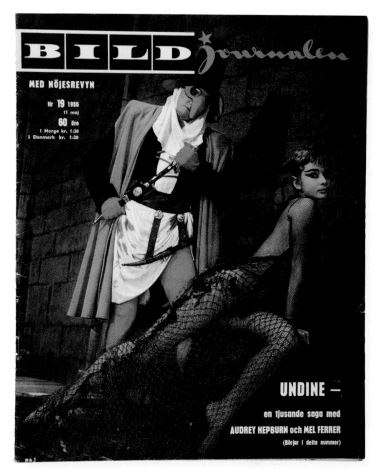

THEATRE ARTS, United States, June 1954

BILD JOURNALEN, Denmark, 1955

EPOCA, Italy, May 16, 1954

THE PLAYBILL, United States, 1954
U.S. theatrical program for Broadway's Ondine.

DIE FILMWOCHE, Germany, Apr. 10, 1954

ORIZZONTI, Italy, Jan. 16, 1955
Striking image showcasing the "imperfections" of Audrey's face, her lamentations about which are frequently quoted.

HOLLYWOOD ROMANCES, United States, 1954

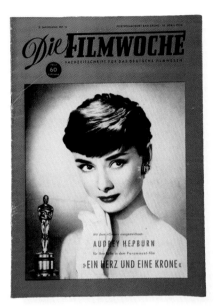

...but should a healthy love strip your nerves?

dren (Chuca Mala, 11, and Christopher, 10); then Mel was divorced from his second wife, and remarried first wife Frances. He and she—first and third wife, Frances—have a son, Mark, 9 years old. This rather complicated personal life Ferrer refers to as "very unconventional conventionality." Professionally, he's been writer, actor, dancer, director, producer. He and Frances, who separated frequently, even after their second marriage, were just about newly reconciled (he'd taken an apartment for the family in New York) when he went into rehearsal for *Ondine*. But the ways of fate are strange, and Frances Ferrer is a woman who knows when she's finally licked. Her husband and Audrey Hepburn lit up the streets around them, whenever they were together. So Frances Ferrer took herself to Mexico, and divorced Mel for the second time. But what about Audrey, and her risky romance? People wondered, and watched. Audrey and Mel digging cool jazz at Birdland. Audrey and Mel doing a hot rhumba at El Morocco. Audrey and Mel rehearsing in a corner of Dinty Moore's. Audrey and Mel letting their ice cream melt as they gazed at each other in Rumpelmayer's. Audrey and

Mel at lunch, and Audrey and Mel at dinner, and Audrey's contract saying if Mel quit the show, she could quit too. And was it possible? This, from the girl whose one aim was to be a great star? Audrey's mother didn't like the affair, so for the first time Audrey stopped listening to her mother. Yet Audrey didn't seem to grow, to flower, to bloom with love. Rather, she seemed near to nervous collapse. Her work schedule could be blamed in part, of course. She hadn't rested in too long a time. But could part of the strain also be blamed on her romance? Walter Winchell thought so, and said so. "Insiders suspect," wrote WW, "that Mel Ferrer is the chief reason Audrey Hepburn's worn out. They're in love." Comes a new question: should a healthy love strip the nerves and make you taut? If Mel cherished the girl, and didn't merely want to be seen in public with America's newest darling, why didn't he keep her home once in a while? Why the desperate rug-cutting all over town? Audrey's conflicts, far from resolving themselves, seemed to be increasing. The charmer everyone loved seemed to be heading straight for trouble, and nobody knew—or knows—how to stop her.

everybody has you madly in love with Mel *he's balding, a lot older, and furthermore he's been married four times before* *as a matter of fact he has four children* *your mother disapproves; the rest of us wonder if you've given your heart time to think it over*

more

BILD Journalen

MED NÖJESREVYN

Nr **37** 1954
9 sept.

60 öre

I Norge kr. 1:20
I Danmark kr. 1:20

Bj med
AUDREY HEPBURN
i Schweiz

(Se sid. 3—5)

Onderonsje met haar echtgenoot Mel Ferrer.

„Over die vraag moet ik even nadenken."

„Mijn grootste vreugde? Mijn man!"
(Onder) „Zie ik er dan zo verveeld uit?"

Un mariage romantique
AUDREY HEPBURN EPOUSE MEL FERRER
(Voir pages 12 et 13)

IDUN

Ung kärlek
Brinnande kärlek
Medelålders kärlek

Nygifta Audrey Hepburn
och Mel Ferrer

Nr 41
Pris 55 öre

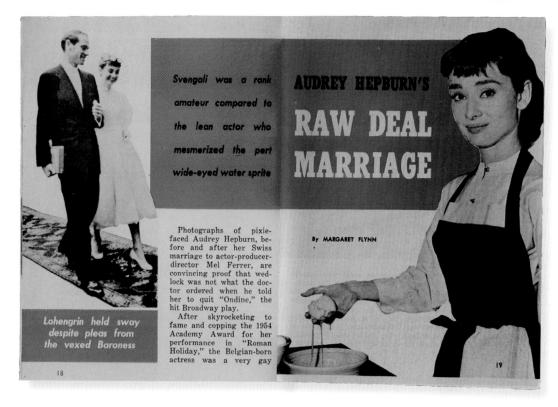

Svengali was a rank amateur compared to the lean actor who mesmerized the pert wide-eyed water sprite

AUDREY HEPBURN'S
RAW DEAL MARRIAGE

By MARGARET FLYNN

Lohengrin held sway despite pleas from the vexed Baroness

Photographs of pixie-faced Audrey Hepburn, before and after her Swiss marriage to actor-producer-director Mel Ferrer, are convincing proof that wedlock was not what the doctor ordered when he told her to quit "Ondine," the hit Broadway play.

After skyrocketing to fame and copping the 1954 Academy Award for her performance in "Roman Holiday," the Belgian-born actress was a very gay

18

19

THE INSIDE FACTS:

why AUDREY HEPBURN is wasting away!

This pathetic pixie can't compete with luscious lasses who attract her Mel

BY
ROY GRAHAM

THERE is a mother in this world who, every time she opens the morning paper, asks herself full of forebodings: "Today?" The story she is watching out for would carry the headline: AUDREY AND FERRER SEPARATE. It hasn't appeared yet, but Miss Hepburn's mom is quite certain that it will one of these days.

That would be almost a relief for the lady, for she is worrying about her daughter's physical appearance. "My girl seems to be getting thinner and thinner," she will tell intimates. "That has always been a sign with her that she is heading for trouble."

The Baroness van Heemstra knows her child. She knows that Audrey, for all her frailty, can be as stubborn as a mule. The girl married Melchior Ferrer over her mother's violent objections. And the baroness is afraid that Audrey will now rather go to pieces than admit that she made a mistake.

Is that merely the over-anxiety of a doting parent for whom her daughter was everything she had in life before "that hungry-looking actor" came along and took Audrey away from her? Or are there other symptoms which indicate that the baroness may be right?

In the first few months after their wedding in September 1954, Mel and Audrey seemed a happy couple. They settled down in the 20-room villa "St. Anthony's Vineyard" at Albano, Italy, and enjoyed a leisurely honeymoon. In November of that year, they paid a "state visit" to Holland where Audrey was received like a ruling queen while Mel played calmly and efficiently the role of a prince consort.

But already in the beginning of 1955, those close to the couple began to notice that the honeymoon was over. To be sure, Audrey adored Melchior. "She *has* to adore him if she can stand living with him," her friends would say. But they were not so sure any longer that Mel loved Audrey, at least not in the thoughtful, unselfish manner which grants the partner a life of her own.

"Mel became more and more possessive and domineering," a confidant of the Ferrers told us. "He treated Audrey less as a human being than as some rare animal he had to protect from the crowd in the zoo. He read her mail, took her telephone calls, drafted her contracts, decided whom she was to see or not to see and canceled interviews in her name without asking her. He acted not like a husband but like a custodian."

Audrey soon got tired of that attitude, our informant added. As deeply as she was devoted to Mel, she was too much attached to her personal freedom to submit to Mel's overwhelming ego without a struggle. So she began to speak up, and they had arguments—but she could never win one. When Mel lost his temper—which happened often—he was liable to hit her, as he did one night in a Roman bar. In the end it was always *she* who gave in for the

Just a bony bundle of nerves, the frail Oscar winner has been called "half boy, half girl" by her spouse, who dominates her and makes all her decisions for her.

EXPOSED

Audrey is always fearful that Mel's eye for a buxom babe may start a furious domestic battle.

Pages 76–77:
BILD JOURNALEN, Sweden, Sept. 9, 1954

ABC, Belgium, Nov. 13, 1954
Magazine cover and interior photostrip.

MODAS CORDADAS VIDA FEMININA,
Portugal, Dec. 1, 1954

LE SOIR ILLUSTRE, France, Oct. 7, 1954

IDUN, Sweden, Oct. 11, 1954

INSIDE, United States, May 1955
Audrey's golden period as media darling ended with the press's sour reception to news of her romance with Ondine co-star Mel Ferrer, as seen in the spreads opposite and above. This initiated much hurtful negative publicity not limited to her love life.

EXPOSED, United States, August 1955

CUE, United States, Mar. 27, 1954

POINT DE VUE, France, Oct. 7, 1954
In the chaplet of white roses for her wedding to Mel Ferrer on September 24, 1954.

GLAMOUR, United States, December 1955

GLAMOUR

**HOW TO DRESS FOR
SIX IMPORTANT
CHRISTMAS OCCASIONS**

Shopping

Office Party

Christmas Eve

Church

Christmas Dinner

Holiday Ball

16 PAGE BONUS
90 Quick and Easy Dinners for 1956
with Special Tips to Make Them Your Own

December, 35 cents

**AUDREY
HEPBURN**
Looks at

WAR AND PEACE

1956

THE RIGHTS TO TOLSTOY'S 1869 NOVEL *War and Peace* had been secured by several aspiring film producers over the decades dating back to the silent film era. With the exception of the Russian production of 1916, prohibitive cost estimates had caused filmmakers to abandon the idea with nothing committed to celluloid. However, three major producers with plenty of backing, Mike Todd and the team of Carlo Ponti and Dino De Laurentiis, decided independently in 1955 that the time was right and that Audrey Hepburn was the star that could make the enterprise profitable. Both parties approached Audrey, but the Ponti–De Laurentiis team won the day by having already offered one of the leading male roles to her husband, Mel.

The project was an ambitious departure for Audrey—a period epic based on a literary classic—but the producers and the director, King Vidor, were not after Tolstoy's literary profundity. They were after a commercial and profitable spectacular in the mold of David O. Selznick's *Gone with the Wind*.

Pregnant late in 1954, Audrey accepted the offer to play Natasha for Ponti–De Laurentiis. Her contract stipulated that her shooting would begin after the baby was born. There were additional benefits: the relatively short distance from her home in Switzerland to Cinecittà's film studios in Rome, the then-record salary of $350,000 for three months' work (plus $500 a week for expenses), and the opportunity to work with her husband. Production began by filming battle scenes in Yugoslavia. While Ferrer was in London shooting *Oh . . . Rosalinda!!*, Audrey settled in to read *War and Peace* at home in Switzerland. Unfortunately, her pregnancy ended in miscarriage in March of 1955.

The film, released in 1956, was not as successful critically as it was commercially. *Time* magazine's fair assessment of the performances was: "What is lacking is the steely courage that would let Natasha brand her flesh with a red-hot iron to prove her love. Instead of a total commitment to life, there is more often a quiet acceptance of fate. Mel Ferrer's Prince Andrei has a certain sullen grandeur, but his diction is often unclear, and he is more wooden than reserved, more testy than proud."

Regarding Audrey's immense talent, *War and Peace* co-star Henry Fonda told journalist Curtis Pepper in *Glamour*, December 1955, "How does she get it? Where does it come from? This little thing. And let's face it, not a lot of experience." King Vidor, a forty-year veteran of Hollywood when he directed Audrey in *War and Peace*, put it this way: "You just say the word and she knows how to draw up the emotion. Don't ask 'em where it comes from. She knows how to find it like somebody on a ranch telling you the water's over there. You say, 'How do you know?' and they tell you, 'Because it's over there.'" Among the kind reviews singling out Audrey was that by British *Films in Review* "[Hepburn] dominates an epic picture by refusing to distort her character to the epic mould [sic], letting her . . . very littleness in the face of history captivate us by its humanity contrasted with the inhumanity of war. She incarnates all that is worth fighting for."

Despite the high profile of the production, the meticulous period costumes designed by Maria De Matteis naturally did not affect contemporary fashion. Nevertheless, Audrey's popularity as a fashion icon remained vibrant; in 1955 and 1956 both her on- and off-screen images persisted on magazines covers throughout the world.

parade

The Sunday Courier and Press
EVANSVILLE, INDIANA

AUDREY HEPBURN:
d's highest-paid actress
SEE PAGE 10

**BE YOU
OWN BUILDE**
. . . a special feature: how
get more house for less mon
SEE PAGE

Page 85:

PARADE, United States, Aug. 21, 1955

NOVELLA, Italy, May 8, 1955

CINEMA NUOVO, Italy, Jul. 25, 1956
Probably taken seconds apart at a publicity function, compare this Cinema Nuovo *image, which captures a calm and alluring sophisticate, to the seemingly distracted neophyte with imperfect teeth on the cover of* Incom Illustrata *at lower left.*

REVUE, Germany, Jun. 4, 1955

PICTURE POST, England, Sept. 3, 1955

INCOM ILLUSTRATA, Italy, Apr. 30, 1955

EVERYBODY'S, England, Feb. 12, 1955

SHEET MUSIC, Australia, 1956
Australian sheet music cover for the Nino Rota theme.

PICTURE SHOW ANNUAL, England, 1957

TANZ ILLUSTRIERTE, Germany, April 1957

NOVELLE FILM, Italy, Nov. 10, 1956

88

LECTURES D'AUJOURD'HUI, Belgium,
Sept. 22, 1956

PARIS MATCH, France, Jun. 4, 1955

CAHIERS DU CINÉMA, France, March 1957

JOURS DE FRANCE, France, Sept. 24, 1955

CONSTANZE, Germany, May 22, 1962

LE ORE, Italy, Nov. 17, 1956

LE ORE

IV 184 SETTIMANALE DI ATTUALITÀ
MILANO, 17 NOVEMBRE 1956

LA STORIA FOTOGRAFICA DEI

DIECI GIORNI
CHE SCONVOLSERO
IL MONDO

DA BUDAPEST

CONTRO I CARRI
COMBATTONO
I RAGAZZI DI
VIA PÄL

80 LIRE

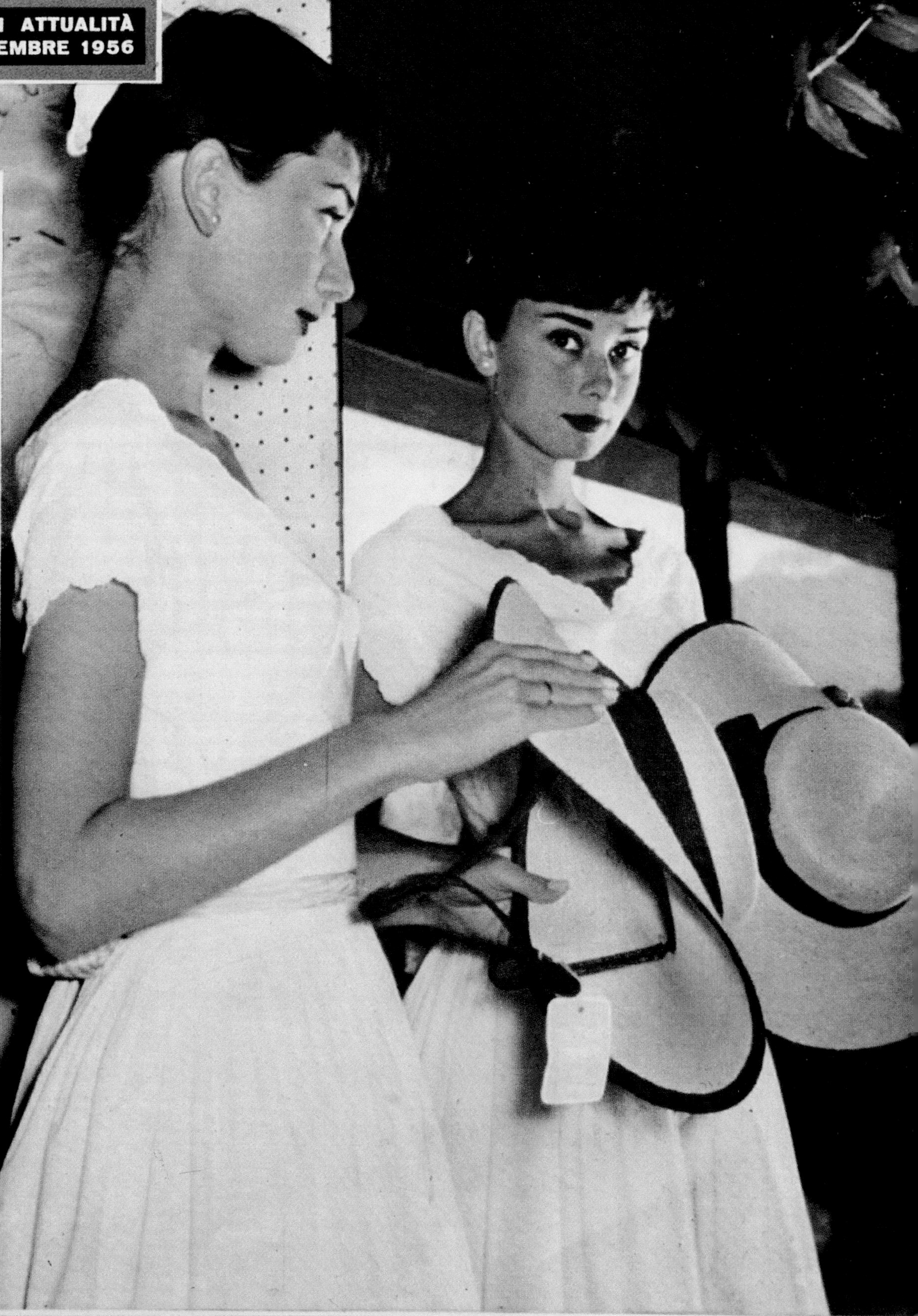

DICE ADDIO A SABRINA L'ULTIMA

AUDREY HEPBURN

PICTURE POST, England, Nov. 5, 1956

FLAMA, Spain, Sept. 14, 1956

ZEPHYR, Greece, 1957

FESTIVAL, France, June 1957

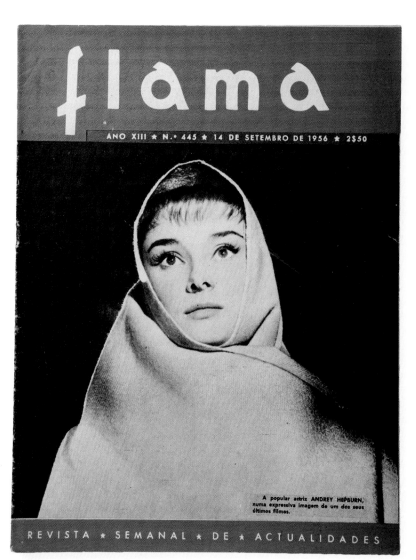

POINT DE VUE, France, Aug. 24, 1956
SILVER SCREEN, United States, December 1956
O CRUZEIRO, Brazil, May 26, 1956
REDBOOK, United States, July 1956
INCOM ILLUSTRATA, Italy, Mar. 10, 1956

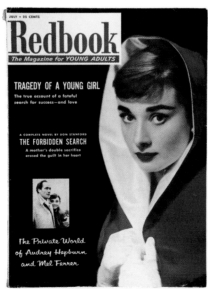

LIFE, United States, Aug. 20, 1956

JOURS DE FRANCE, France, June 1957

CINÉ REVUE, France, Nov. 30, 1956

NEWSWEEK, United States, Jul. 30, 1956

HEMMETS VECKOTIDNING, Sweden, Dec. 14, 1955

EPOCA, Italy, Jul. 11, 1955

OUR WORLD, Israel, August 1956

UUTISAITTA, Finland, 1957

OGGI, Italy, Mar. 15, 1956
Audrey's stern profile and poised riding crop tantalize from this publicity photo for War and Peace.

VECKO-TIDNINGEN SÅNINGSMANNEN,
Aug. 18, 1956

WAR AND PEACE PROGRAM, Japan, 1956

DE POST, Netherlands, Apr. 15, 1956

POST

t weekblad dat C op de hoogte houdt

Jaargang - N° 15 - 15 april 1956

elgië 7,50 Fr. - Nederland 55 Ct

Het zilveren huwelijksfeest

van de graaf en gravin van Parijs werd een gebeurtenis (Exclusieve foto's)

★

God woont ook in beton

Kunnen wij kerken bouwen, die ons geloofsleven belichamen ?

★

Audrey Hepburn speelt Tolstoi's Oorlog en Vrede

★

Foto voorpagina :
Audrey Hepburn als Natasja.

FUNNY FACE

1957

FUNNY FACE WAS A CLASSIC MGM MUSICAL MADE at Paramount, part of an arrangement between the two to bring Paramount's foremost star, Audrey Hepburn, into a project that already included MGM's Fred Astaire. The production originated in 1947, a creation of playwright and lyricist Leonard Gershe, friend of *Harper's Bazaar* and *Vogue* photographer Richard Avedon. Gershe had told his friend Clemence Dane the story of how Avedon had made his wife Doe into a top model despite her disinterest in the career. Dane's response reportedly had been, "What a glorious idea for a musical—the fashion world, a fashion photographer, and a model who doesn't want to be a model. Why don't you write it?"

On Dane's advice, Gershe wrote a stage libretto in which Avedon and his wife were thinly veiled as Rick and Jo, and created another character inspired by *Harper's Bazaar* editor in chief Diana Vreeland. It was offered to MGM's Roger Edens under the title *Wedding Day.* Apparently Edens liked the play, but not the score (by Vernon Duke and Ogden Nash). As legend has it, Edens noted the line Gershe had written for the Jo Stockton character, "I think my face is perfectly funny," and suggested the Gershwin song "Funny Face" from the musical of the same name, be included. Eventually, rights to the title and contents of the entire 1927 stage production of *Funny Face* were purchased, the property was dismantled, and the title and song "Funny Face" were transposed into the otherwise unrelated film.

When Edens and Gershe learned that Audrey Hepburn, the most sought-after star in Hollywood, was a dancer and wanted to do a musical, they immediately sent her the script.

Audrey was quoted at the time as saying that she "fell in love with it," but later admitted that the deciding factor had been to "experience the thrill that all women at some point in their lives have dreamed of—to dance, just once, with Fred Astaire." And the project put Astaire in his natural element performing Gershwin songs, as he had memorably in the original *Funny Face* and in *A Damsel in Distress* and *Shall We Dance.*

Negotiations were complicated partly because Audrey's agent, Kurt Frings, dictated demanding financial conditions, and required other special accommodations arguably appropriate to the most sought-after star in Hollywood. One was that, although Edith Head had been assigned to the film, Hubert de Givenchy be provided with a copy of the script. Unlike the arrangement for *Sabrina,* Givenchy would design clothes expressly for *Funny Face.* Credits would boldly proclaim "Miss Hepburn's Paris Wardrobe by Hubert de Givenchy." Although this credit implies that Audrey's New York beatnik clothes had been designed by Edith Head, director Stanley Donen, according to David Chierichetti in *Edith Head: The Life and Times of Hollywood's Celebrated Costume Designer* (2003), "remembers that even those were Givenchy's. What he did was to make female versions of the drab clothes he habitually wore himself. The black slacks she wore in the 'Basal Metabolism' number came from Jax in Beverly Hills, and the matter of her white socks in that number was one settled by Hepburn and Donen themselves without any input from Edith. Even Kay Thompson's camel-hair coat in the 'Bonjour Paris' number . . . was Givenchy's." The French designer was given film credit for his gowns in *Funny Face* and the recognition now gave Audrey great satisfaction. After 1957, Audrey's film contracts would include a clause that wherever suitable, "clothes by Givenchy."

Regarding Audrey's famous and influential outfit for the "Basal Metabolism" beatnik dance number, director Stanley Donen later recalled, "Audrey and I agreed she would wear black, tight-fitting pants, a black sweater, and black shoes. I wanted her to wear white socks with it and she was stunned. 'Absolutely not!' she said. 'It will spoil the whole black silhouette and cut the line at my feet!' I said, 'If you don't wear the white socks you will fade into the background, there will be no definition to your movement, and the dance sequence will be bland and dull.' She burst into tears and ran into her dressing room. After a little while she regained her composure, put on the white socks, returned to the set, and went ahead without a whimper. Later, when she saw the sequence, she sent me a note saying, 'You were right about the socks. Love, Audrey.' "

Another measure of Audrey's position in Hollywood was that she, a veteran of just three major films, was granted top credit billing over Astaire, veteran of twenty-seven, and for whom the project was at first being customized as a starring vehicle. Audrey had arrived.

The resulting film, though the sum of some splendid parts, is a mess. Audrey came aboard a project that was being developed as an Astaire vehicle on the basis of her star power rather than because of the appropriateness of the casting. (There are awkward differences in Audrey's and Astaire's performing styles—his hammy, hers nuanced—and ages; critic Pauline Kael pointed out that the film "emphasizes Astaire's age by trying to ignore it.") The freighting in of nostalgic, unrelated Gershwin songs that make sense only in an Astaire vehicle hopelessly dates the film. There's also the irking presumption that a bookish student of philosophy would be a pushover for superficial redemption by a self-absorbed, two-dimensional Lothario; and the sexist and anti-intellectual premise that a pretty girl who ignores fashion needs male mentorship to fulfill her "potential." There's also some remedial and puritanical jabbing at the contemporary existentialist beatnik scene.

But with all of that considerable lot aside, the film features beautiful art direction by Avedon, particularly evident during the opening credits, the initial New York scenes, and the Paris fashion shoots; the production is a wonderful imitation (utilizing MGM production staff on loan between the studios) of the grand MGM–musical style; the wardrobe by Givenchy is brilliant; and, of course, there's Audrey.

DAMERNAS VÄRLD, Sweden, Jun. 27, 1957

PARIS MATCH, France, Mar. 3, 1956

DAMERNAS VÄRLD, Sweden, Apr. 12, 1956

DAMERNAS

värld

Nr 14 1956
5—12 april
Pris **55** öre

Norge 1:10
Danmark 1:10

Ni som går i giftastankar...

se sid. 21 och sid. 42—48

MARIE CLAIRE, France, September 1956

O CRUZEIRO, Brazil, Jul. 16, 1957

COSMOPOLITAN, United States, February 1957

HAYAT, Turkey, Sept. 20, 1957
*Audrey demonstrates her inborn sense of style as she
transforms a gingham picnic napkin into a soigné chapeau.*

STAR REVUE, Germany, 1957

PICCOLO, Netherlands, 1957

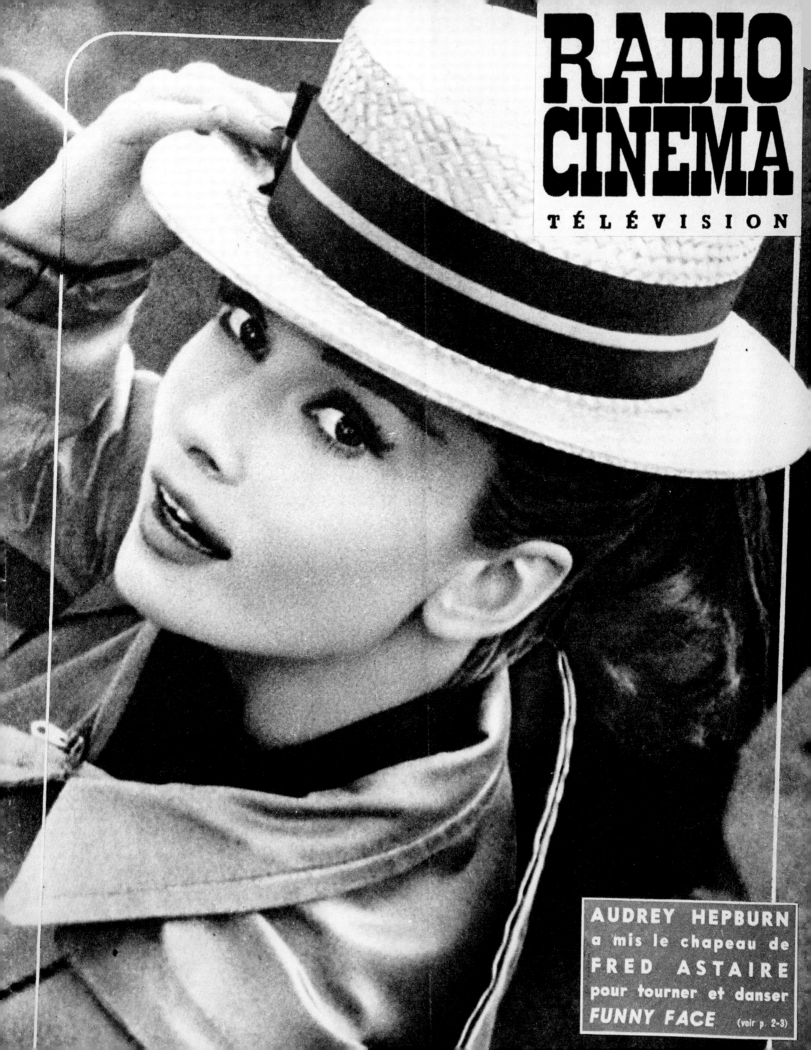

RADIO CINEMA

TÉLÉVISION

AUDREY HEPBURN
a mis le chapeau de
FRED ASTAIRE
pour tourner et danser
FUNNY FACE (voir p. 2-3)

RADIO CINEMA TÉLÉVISION, France, Jul. 8, 1956

LECTURAS, Spain, Feb. 15, 1958

VECKO JOURNALEN, Sweden, Jul. 28, 1956

EIGA NO TOMO, Japan, August 1957

AUDREY HEPBURN, Portugal, 1957

COSMOPOLITAN, United States, February 1957
Cosmopolitan *magazine ridicules the superficiality of*
Funny Face *through their article's mocking title.*

HARPER'S BAZAAR, United States, April 1956

HARPER'S BAZAAR, United States, October 1956

A Photographer and His Model Make a Pretty Movie

Dick Avedon, whose real life adventures inspired Paramount film "Funny Face" steps behind his camera for a special Cosmopolitan sneak prevue of Audrey Hepburn as waif-turned-fashion-model

TEXT BY PEGGY COOK   PHOTOS BY RICHARD AVEDON

Whisked out of her dowdy Greenwich Village bookshop and into the world of high fashion, Audrey Hepburn—in her latest Paramount picture—is transformed from a cotton-stockinged bookworm into a chiffon-gowned "Quality Woman." The stunt is the brainchild of "Quality" Magazine editor Kay ("Eloise") Thompson, whose aim is to boost her intellectual readers' interest in clothes, and the magazine's circulation as well. To her crack photographer (Fred Astaire) Editor Thompson gives the assignment of finding this "Quality Woman" (who must have brains as well as beauty), of escorting her to Paris, and of photographing her for a fashion scoop.

The movie, "Funny Face," has no connection with the show of the same name which played on Broadway a few years back. It does, however, revive several tunes Gershwin wrote for the stage show, including the title song and "'S Wonderful," "How Long Has This Been Going On?" and "Clap Yo' Hands." To these author Leonard Gershe and producer Roger Edens added such production numbers as "Think Pink," "Bonjour, Paris" and "On How to Be Lovely," in which Audrey realizes a longstanding desire to return to her first love, the dance.

Writer Gershe met top-flight fashion photographer Richard Avedon when both were serving in the Merchant

50

Marine, and he decided that Avedon's life was meat for a musical comedy. The original show (then titled "Wedding Day") was headed for Broadway when M-G-M bought the screen rights and added the Gershwin score. Then Paramount offered Audrey Hepburn as leading lady and the entire production moved to that studio.

Cast and crew were transported to Paris for the filming, and real-life backdrops include the Eiffel Tower, Champs-Elysees, Montmartre, the moonlit gardens at Versailles, and a Left Bank basement bistro. Miss Hepburn's extensive wardrobe is by Givenchy, who happens to be her own personal couturier.

Photographer Avedon was content to limit his participation in the film to "visual consultant"; nevertheless, he consented to step into Fred Astaire's role for this special Cosmopolitan prevue of "Funny Face." On the next three pages are the results of his Pygmalion venture.

(continued)

THE BOOKWORM TURNS *into a picture of fashion elegance when editor, designer, photographer join forces in "Funny Face." Givenchy draped white chiffon over a black sheath; the toque: sheared white beaver*

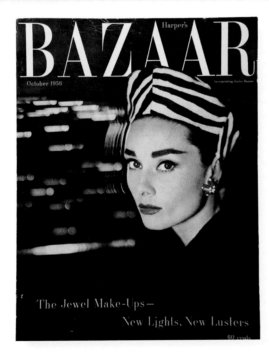

Win a Don Loper Wardrobe

teenage
BEAUTY
AND FASHION PREVIEW

50¢

RENSART
CDC

TEEN MODELING
"the Loretta
Young way"

Teen Fashion Guide

"Find Your Face"
BY BUD WESTMORE

the secret of
NATALIE WOOD'S
popularity

how-to
HAIR STYLES

A COMPLETE GUIDE TO CLEAR SKIN

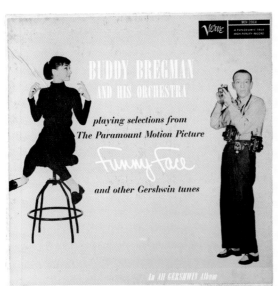

TEENAGE BEAUTY, United States, 1957
A fine example of Audrey's theatrical modeling acumen. With the outfit's collar turned down, she's an ingénue, with collar up, a vamp.

ORIGINAL SOUNDTRACK RECORDING,
United States, 1957

LOBBY CARDS, United States, 1957
Two theater lobby cards showcase the action during the beatnik dance number "Basal Metabolism" from Funny Face. *White socks with an otherwise black outfit was suggested by Billy Wilder, and was at first resisted by Audrey. The look would be influential decades later through its adoption by Michael Jackson.*

BUDDY BREGMAN AND HIS ORCHESTRA ALBUM,
United States, 1957

SUNDAY MIRROR, United States, Apr. 21, 1957

HARPER'S BAZAAR, United States, May 1957
*For its third cover feature on Audrey in thirteen months,
Bazaar gleefully rolls out seven more pages of Audrey
in Givenchy to celebrate the arrival of fashion forward
Funny Face.*

NOVELLA, Italy, Nov. 4, 1957
*Audrey signs publicity photos on set location for Funny
Face at a country churchyard in Chantilly, France. The
wedding gown was designed by Givenchy for the film's
romantic finale.*

HARPER'S BAZAAR, United States, May 1957
*A film not just including current fashion, but about
fashion industry people, couldn't help but enjoy
extravagant promotion in the major fashion magazines
of the day.*

RICHARD AVEDON

Car Coats —

● Above: That rainy-day classic,
the mackintosh, looking the brighter
for the print it opens on.
It's made of Reeves' waterproof cotton
twill; the lining is rayon surah;
the model (both pages),
Audrey Hepburn, re-enacting
for *Harper's Bazaar* her role
in *Funny Face*. Coat by Modelia.
About $35, Bonwit Teller;
Kaufmann's; I. Magnin.
Gloves by Grandoe; Mark Cross umbrella.

RICHARD AVEDON

Summer Cottons —

● Summer will breeze right *through*
this summery new cotton,
and vice versa—it's green-and-white
checked gingham, with a fragile,
floating air woven right in
at the loom. The dress,
like the gingham itself,
is designed for ease
and breeziness. By Mollie Parnis,
in Dumari Pima cotton. About $80.
(For stores, see opposite page.)
The bandeau, in a matching gingham, by Madcaps.

LOVE IN THE AFTERNOON

1957

and MAYERLING

AUDREY'S MANAGER KURT FRINGS ADVISED HER not to get involved with *Love in the Afternoon.* She chose to do so at the behest of its director, Billy Wilder, whom Audrey had grown to admire when they worked together on *Sabrina* just two years earlier. Originally titled Ariane, this French bedroom comedy had received screen treatment twice before, first in the 1931 German production *Ariane,* then again the following year in a French offering *Jeune Fille Russe.* The plot concerns an innocent young girl, Ariane, who wins over a roguish, middle-aged playboy by feigning a romantic past the equal of his—and through this disingenuous seduction, she eventually reforms him. In *Love in the Afternoon,* Audrey's authentically youthful Ariane appeared plausibly virginal; in both prior movies, however, ostensibly vestal, middle-aged Arianes reforming older playboys strained the credulity of viewers and critics. Unfortunately, Audrey's co-star, Gary Cooper—three decades Audrey's senior and not aging in the burnished way that might have suited the plot—gave the new adaptation a different incredulous spin. The age gap seems particularly awkward when seen today. Even at the time, a *Newsweek* review declaimed: "The allure of the movie depends almost entirely on the allure of these three institutionalized film personalities [Hepburn, Cooper and Chevalier]. After a time, even the most loyal fan is apt to wish for a change of face, of place and particularly of pace."

The allure of the film for Audrey, or for director Wilder, is unclear. Several factors probably contributed. In adapting Claude Genet's already quaint, thirty-year-old play for the commercially stumbling Allied Artists Pictures Corporation, Wilder was supporting the studio's attempt to revive itself by enlisting top directors and actors in otherwise low-budget projects. The back-to-basics approach might have appealed to Audrey in light of her husband's commitment to theater; the convenience of the European location helped; and her dedication to Wilder sealed the deal.

Audrey, still in her twenties, once more performed opposite a man old enough to be her father. Billy Wilder originally pursued fifty-two-year-old Cary Grant, and then forty-one-year-old Yul Brynner; but both declined, the former gracefully regarding himself as too old for the role, the latter bound by scheduling conflicts. The poignant uplift of a story in which naive, youthful exuberance wins over jaded privilege was unfortunately lost in the miscasting of Cooper. The film's often corny dialogue and running time of more than two hours also didn't help. Successful recruitment of Yul Brynner might have resulted in a more energetic and sexier vehicle for Audrey.

According to Hubert de Givenchy, his designs are featured in *Love in the Afternoon,* even though no wardrobe designer is officially credited on the released print. It is likely that Givenchy was not credited because, as with *Sabrina,* he had not been commissioned to create specific designs for the film. Rather, Audrey probably chose her own wardrobe from an existing collection at the House of Givenchy near Parc Monceau in Paris, where by this time she was an inveterate regular. The couture in this film was low key for the most part, and is very rarely discussed. While in *Sabrina,* the simplified backgrounds and black and white cinematography flatter the wardrobe design, in *Love in the Afternoon,* the wardrobe competes unfavorably with ornate baroque sets in widescreen VistaVision.

The film features a few trademark Givenchy designs, including another boatneck dress, this time a white print with mid-calf-length, draped skirt, accessorized with black bag, white gloves, and low heels. Two additional distinctly Givenchy designs are a white, ruffled, calf-length, flared cocktail dress with a large frontal bow at the waist with which was worn a white satin bolero jacket with three-quarter length sleeves, matching white satin pumps, hair ribbon, and quarter-length white gloves; and a double-breasted, wool coat with exaggerated big buttons that foreshadowed a '60s vogue.

Lyricist Alan Jay Lerner visited Maurice Chevalier and Audrey Hepburn on the set of *Love in the Afternoon* to offer them the lead roles in the musical adaptation of Colette's *Gigi* he was developing with Frederick Loewe. Audrey had successfully introduced a non-musical *Gigi* to American theater audiences in her 1952 New York debut. The musical seemed a logical move. However, Audrey declined the lucrative offer, saying that she believed herself too old at twenty-eight to pass for a teenager. The film, starring Leslie Caron (age twenty-six) and Maurice Chevalier, went on to become one of the most successful musical films of all time. Audrey chose instead to work with her husband on *Mayerling,* an all but forgotten footnote to her career.

Mayerling was an adaptation of Claude Anet's 1930 novel *Idyll's End,* based on the true story of Austria's Prince Rudolf and his mistress, Baroness Mary Vetsera. Both had been found dead in mysterious circumstances in the prince's Viennese hunting lodge, in what the Anet retelling supposes was a double suicide. The daring ninety-minute, live television performance, which included ten costume changes for Audrey, was filmed and broadcast in color (unusual at the time) to accentuate the impressive sets and elaborate period wardrobe by Dorothy Jeakins. The production, boasting a budget of over $600,000, extraordinary for television at that time, bore some visual resemblance to *War and Peace.* The director and producer, Anatole Litvak, friend of the Ferrers, was also responsible for the honored original 1936 French film adaptation. Understandably, expectations ran high for this star-studded reworking. Unfortunately, the ambitious project was not well received. Columnist and TV critic John Crosby said, "The lovers seemed more fated to bore each other to death than to end their illicit alliance in a murder-suicide pact."

WIENER ILLUSTRIERTE, Austria, Dec. 19, 1959

ELOKUVA-AITTA, Finland, July 1958

NEW SCREEN NEWS, Australia, Nov. 15, 1957

Left and facing page: Magazine cover and spread. If this article's title, "New Hepburn Cut Leads To Fashion," was ever accurate in Australia it would indeed have been news. Though the coiffeur from Love in the Afternoon *received much early exposure due to the fashion momentum established by Audrey's previous films, the style never actually caught on.*

Summer Hairdo

New Hepburn Cut Leads

Remember the Italian cut, the Sabrina and Natasha cuts. They were all introduced into the world of hair styles by actress Audrey Hepburn and quickly adapted or copied by fashion-conscious girls the world over.

Now Audrey has introduced a new cut, designed with those hot summer days in mind and featured in her latest movie, "Love in the Afternoon."

High, wide and handsome, cool, comfortable and exciting, the "Ariane" is convertible. Four different styles to match Milady's mood and all designed to create excitement at the office, cocktails, evening or under the summer sun.

For shopping or the office and all informal or semi-informal occasions, Audrey (left and below) has introduced this variation of the page-boy cut. The hair is brushed back loosely and the ends are gently turned under.

In the original cutting for all these styles, the hair is snipped at an even length, with approximately three inches at the top and two inches at the temple area. The length at the nape is about four inches.

In setting for this style, Audrey extends part in the centre three inches back from the forehead, sections hair on either side of the part and turns under on rollers. Fullness of the front is brushed practically out and the bangs brushed back. The hair is then brushed under in soft wavy page-boy style.

The Fashion

A very formal evening occasion demands more attention and Audrey (right) makes a variation to create a bouffant effect. The hair is first brushed back close to the head and repeated by comb and hand; then sprayed lightly. It is then combed back into page boy and the bangs combed forward over hand. Ribbon or clip holds directly behind bangs. A third variation (not pictured) puts the hair completely up and makes an ideal style for cocktail time.

Audrey wears all four styles in the film to create the right atmosphere and the character of the girl she plays. "When the audience first sees Ariane (the character I play), I'm sure they'll know immediately just what type of girl she is," says Audrey.

Strictly for the outdoors, holidays or week-ends is the fourth variation (below), which tends to take years off any girl's age. Audrey parts on the left and sleekly brushes back on each side to form pigtails which are tied with ribbon. The top falls loosely over the forehead to form a side bang.

This new Ariane cut, which is named after the character Audrey plays in the film, is currently the rage in America and even at this stage is starting to spread to the Continent.

In "Love in the Afternoon," Audrey plays a petite French lass who has been sheltered from the hard facts of life by her private detective father (Maurice Chevalier), but is suddenly awakened into full womanhood by an internationally infamous rumeo (Gary Cooper). Played strictly for comedy, with a slight tingle of blue, the movie is comparable and easily equal to "The Moon is Blue." And it should be just as popular.

NEW SCREEN NEWS
Page 4 — Nov. 15, 1957

NEW SCREEN NEWS
Page 5 — Nov. 15, 1957

REVUE, Germany, Jun. 1, 1957

CINÉMONDE, France, Feb. 7, 1957

AJAN SAVEL, Finland, June 1958

STAR REVUE, Germany, May 1959

MARGRIET, Belgium, Feb. 16, 1957

KUVA-POSTI, Finland, Oct. 18, 1956

HJEMMET, Denmark, Nov. 27, 1956

EPOCA, Italy, Oct. 21, 1956

FILM IDEAL

N.º 13 - NOVIEMBRE 1957 - 7 PTAS.

FILM IDEAL, Spain, November 1957

RADIO CINEMA TÉLÉVISION, France, Sept. 23, 1958

OGGI, Italy, Sept. 13, 1956

LE FILM COMPLET, France, Oct. 24, 1957

Cary Grant had declined the role because he believed himself too old to be the love interest of twenty-eight-year-old Audrey Hepburn, so the role of playboy Frank Flannagan passed to the even older, and evidently less discriminating, Gary Cooper.

ECRAN, Chile, Nov. 4, 1958
With her beloved pet, Famous of Hassam.

EPOCA, Italy, May 18, 1958

FILM REVUE, Germany, May 13, 1958

LADIES HOME COMPANION, United States, November 1963

FILM UND FRAU, Germany, 1957
SCREEN, Japan, February 1961

PICCOLO, Belgium, Feb. 22, 1959

STARS PARADE, Thailand, 1958

AJAN SAVEL, Finland, January 1958

HEMMETS VECKOTIDNING, Sweden, May 4, 1959

MARIE CLAIRE, France, May 1957

*Such was Audrey's fashion status by this point in 1957 that
Marie Claire featured a cover story and profuse photo-laden
multi-page article on the making of* Mayerling *even though
the production utilized only period costumes.*

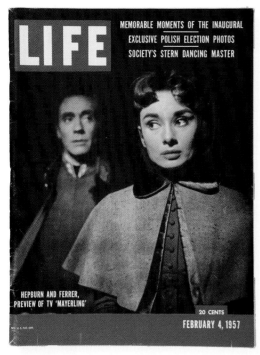

IDUN, Sweden, Jan. 21, 1957

EPOCA, Italy, Jun. 23, 1957

LIFE, United States, Feb. 4, 1957
Cover and full-page ad in the magazine (opposite) for
Mayerling, *the first made-for-television movie shot on
a theater-film's budget.*

Audrey Hepburn and Mel Ferrer make their color TV
debut in "Mayerling," produced, directed and staged
by Anatole Litvak. See this absorbing, true story of
Archduke Rudolph's star-crossed love affair—Mon-
day, February 4, 8:00-9:30 pm, EST, on Producers'
Showcase. 90 minutes, live, in color and black-and-
white on NBC COLOR TELEVISION   a service of RCA

STAR, Thailand, 1957

PARADE, United States, Feb. 17, 1957

ÖĞLEDEN SONRA, Turkey, August 1958

ORIGINAL SOUNDTRACK, United States, 1957
Verve Records extended play 7" record featuring instrumental music from Love in the Afternoon.

THE NUN'S STORY

1959

AFTER A NUMBER OF PROJECTS THAT SHE PURSUED for practical and circumstantial reasons, *The Nun's Story* offered Audrey a chance to work on material closer to her heart and personal experience. The film was adapted from Kathryn C. Hulme's 1956 novel, based on the true story of Marie-Louise Habets, a headstrong Belgian woman who left the religious life after seventeen years at the height of World War II to "fight evil" more directly by participating in the Dutch Resistance. To the studios, the story seemed patently non-commercial without the unlikely participation of a major star—most of the screenplay is devoted to the labors and sacrifices involved in entering Roman Catholic religious order.

The role turned out to be pivotal in the evolution of Audrey's public image, although it might have been a questionable career move for most stars. Publicly, the role of a singularly scrupulous nun cemented her image, particularly with women, as a model of goodness and propriety—in direct contrast with the overt sex appeal that surrounded most other successful female Hollywood stars of the time.

For Hepburn personally, the parallel with her past working for the Dutch Resistance under Nazi occupation must have been a powerful lure. During the shoot, Mel Ferrer was scheduled to be working on the film *Fraulein* in Germany, a country that Audrey refused to visit after her wartime experiences.

While Audrey would be on her own throughout six months of rigorous work, the production was based in part at familiar Cinecittà film studios in Rome (where *War and Peace* had been filmed), as well as on location in Ghent, Belgium, and what is now Kisangani, Zaire.

The film's director, Fred Zinnemann, wrote in an autobiographical piece for British quarterly *Focus On Film,* "With the exception of Ingrid Bergman, there was at that time no star as incandescent as Audrey. She was shy, coltish, and intelligent; she looked delicate, but there was a hint of iron in the jawline that signified a stubborn will. I thought she would be ideal." Zinnemann's sensitive direction, Franz Planer's brilliant Technicolor cinematography, Robert Anderson's compelling screenplay, and Audrey's "disciplined, gracious [and] dedicated" performance (in Zinnemann's assessment) made this the most uniformly excellent film of Audrey's career.

Stylistically however, it is no surprise that Marjorie Best's meticulous wardrobe designs copying traditional, somber religious garb had no influence on fashion, and Alberto De Rossi's makeup was, of course, minimal. Notwithstanding, Audrey was radiant from within her habit, and there are many lovely photographic images from the making of this film.

Télémonde

Cinémonde

AUDREY HEPBURN, sacrée

CINEMA
Reporter

Audrey Hepburn

No. 1123

Page 133:
TÉLÉMONDE, France, Jan. 26, 1960

CINEMA REPORTER, Mexico, Feb. 27, 1960

PLATEIA, Portugal, Feb. 15, 1958

VIE NUOVE, Italy, Oct. 13, 1959

DE POST, Netherlands, Jun. 29, 1958

FILM REVUE, Germany, 1958
Interior spread from the magazine.

ORIGINAL FILM SCORE, United States, 1959
*Warner Brothers Records LP jacket for the U.S. release
of Franz Waxman's brilliant score for* The Nun's Story.

PLATEA, Portugal, Feb. 15, 1958

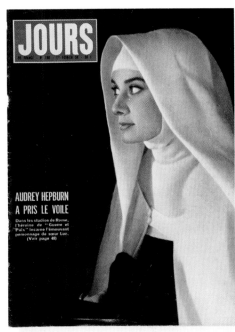

DER STERN, Germany, Nov. 15, 1958

JOURS, France, Feb. 1, 1958

AUDREY HEPBURN MAGAZINE, Spain, 1959
*Spanish fan magazine devoted to the career and life
story of Audrey Hepburn.*

LE PATRIOTE ILLUSTRÉ, France, Feb. 16, 1958

OUTDOOR LIVING

TOWN & COUNTRY

ESTABLISHED 1846

MARCH 1958 PRICE 75 CENTS

AUDREY HEPBURN

TOWN AND COUNTRY, United States, March 1958

ZONDAGSVRIEND, Netherlands, Oct. 2, 1958

INCOM ILLUSTRATA, Italy, Sept. 12, 1959

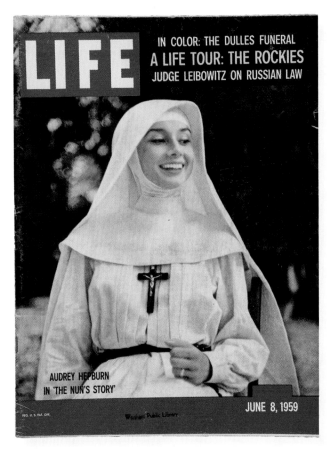

MAGAZINE DO DIARIO ILUSTRADO, Portugal, Feb. 7, 1959

LIFE, United States, Jun. 8, 1959
The Nun's Story helped Audrey, then twenty-eight, shift out of love-struck, girlish roles and into more mature parts, while also solidifying her image as a wholesome role model.

VECO-TIDNINGEN SÅNINGSMANNEN, Sweden, Oct. 3, 1959

LA SEMAINE, Belgium, Nov. 15, 1959

WIENER ILLUSTRIERTE, Austria, January 1958

Wiener Illustrierte

S 2.60

Kein Aschenbrödel mehr
ist das ehemalige Chorgirl Audrey Hepburn. Bei
der Wahl der zehn bestgekleideten Frauen der
Welt eroberte die Oscar-Preisträgerin hinter
Königin Elizabeth einen beachtlichen fünften
Platz. Mehr über die Konkurrenz der Mondänen
auf Seite 5 dieses Blattes.   Foto: UP

GREEN MANSIONS

1959–1960

and THE UNFORGIVEN

OVER THE COURSE OF DECADES, THE RIGHTS FOR W. H. Hudson's 1904 novel *Green Mansions* had been secured by various filmmakers, but the project had been repeatedly shelved as unworkable, or possibly under a curse. MGM screenwriter Dorothy Kingsley offered her adaptation of the classic to Mel Ferrer, who had been searching for a vehicle in which he could direct his wife.

After he completed filming *Fraulein* in Germany, and while Audrey was shooting *The Nun's Story*, Mel scouted suitable locations in South America. Eventually the shooting was done on indoor soundstages at MGM. Since the film was set almost entirely in the forest, the ambiance suffered. One reviewer lamented, "[Audrey] looks as if she had been given an overdose of chlorophyll. In fact the whole thing, even the authentic background footage, has an appalling greenish patina that makes it look as if it had been filmed in a decaying parsley patch."

One film critic summed it up: "Absurd studio bound Shangri La story based on an Edwardian fantasy that may well have suited the printed page, but not the wide screen. Dismally photographed in shades of green, with all concerned looking acutely uncomfortable." The ethereal melodrama of Rima, martyred "Bird Girl" of the South American rain forest, might have worked under best-case direction and production before 1925 as a cultish, mood-lit, silent film; but alas, the 1959 production directed by Mel Ferrer failed utterly.

Green Mansions is an unpopular film, infrequently discussed. It remains unclear why Audrey agreed to do it. One suggestion is that Mel Ferrer favored (for himself and for her) projects based in "literature" above the ostensibly lighter fare in which she shone, and he had encourage this role.

Paramount had only two pictures remaining on their contract with Audrey, and they declined *Green Mansions* and several other projects she had been willing to undertake with her husband, but which were never produced: Thomas Wolfe's *Look Homeward, Angel*; Jean Anouilh's *The Lark* (based on the story of Joan of Arc); Charlotte Bronte's *Jane Eyre*; and Edmond Rostand's play about the life of Napoleon II, *L'Aiglon*. Paramount had given MGM the right to release an Audrey vehicle directed by Ferrer in exchange for Paramount's use of MGM's property (*Funny Face*), contract star (Fred Astaire), and production staff: Paramount shrewdly passed MGM *Green Mansions*.

Green Mansions was produced in 1959, after *The Nun's Story*, but due to the latter's lengthy post-production, it was decided that *Green Mansions* be released first. Dorothy Jeakins, who had designed the wardrobe for Mayerling in 1957, specialized in exotic and period costumes. Other films for which Jeakins designed such costumes were *The Ten Commandments* (1956), *The Sound of Music* (1965), and *Little Big Man* (1970). Audrey would work with Jeakins twice more in her career, in *The Unforgiven* (1960) and *Children's Hour* (1962).

Audrey had promised herself a much-needed vacation after *Green Mansions*. But the temptation of a lucrative opportunity to do a major American western—at a time when the genre was a national craze—and undertake a role of topical gravity proved irresistible, and she signed on to *The Unforgiven* in the late summer of 1958. The film deals with the complexities of racism within a family of white settlers in 1860s Texas. Audrey's character, Rachel, the daughter of the family, is revealed to be a full-blooded Kiowa Indian, who had been rescued as an infant by the family matriarch (Lillian Gish). The film portrays the impact of this revelation upon her heretofore protective, but otherwise headstrong, "Indian fighting" brothers (Burt Lancaster, Doug McClure, and Audie Murphy).

Director John Huston saw the opportunity to make a socially significant film that addressed the critical issue of racism through the lens of historical drama. As Huston said later in his autobiography, *An Open Book*, he regretted that the producers (who included co-star Lancaster) would not assent to intensifying the study of racial intolerance, which was an element of the novel by Alan Le May, but a rarity in Hollywood westerns. Instead, Huston was compelled to make the picture that he "had unfortunately signed on to make when [he] accepted the job in the first place—a swashbuckler about a larger-than-life frontiersman."

The Unforgiven was shot in the sweltering desert of Durango, Mexico, in the spring of 1959. After the strains of location shooting in the Belgian Congo and the faux rain forests at MGM for *The Nun's Story* and *Green Mansions,* and coupled with her anemia, Audrey's health had deteriorated.

During the production of *The Unforgiven,* Audrey mounted Diablo, the white Arabian stallion she rode bareback in the film. Following some disturbance, another horse startled Diablo, who in turn charged, then stopped suddenly, throwing a terrified and screaming Audrey over his head. The accident fractured four of her vertebrae, sprained a foot, tore lower back muscles, and caused hemorrhaging. After Audrey was inside the ambulance, John Huston, Burt Lancaster, and Audie Murphy gathered and looked on with great concern through the rear window. Audrey, in great pain, quipped: "I'm taking a vacation. Want to join me?"

Fortunately, the breaks were clean and did not require surgery, and Audrey was expected to recover in just six weeks. During her recuperation, Marie-Louise Habets, the nun upon whose life *The Nun's Story* was based, volunteered to serve as her personal nurse. When shooting resumed, Audrey wore an orthopedic brace, and traveled prone to and from the set in the back of a station wagon. All concerned knew that the fateful scene with Audrey atop Diabolo would need to be reshot; it was saved until the last scene of the shooting schedule. The second time, it went off without a hitch.

Upon returning home after completion of the film, Audrey, now pregnant, began knitting baby clothes in anticipation. But she again miscarried, setting off what she termed her "black decline." Her weight dropped to ninety pounds, and she was smoking more than three packs of cigarettes per day and fighting off a nervous breakdown. Soon after the Ferrers' fifth wedding anniversary in October 1959, Audrey became pregnant for a third time, and this was cause to clear the calendar so as not to provoke another miscarriage.

This decision derailed Audrey's verbal agreement with Alfred Hitchcock to star in a production called *No Bail for the Judge.* She was to play opposite Laurence Olivier, who would play her father, a judge, and Laurence Harvey as a London barrister charged with the daunting task of defending the judge from a trumped-up murder charge. Without Audrey's participation, both Laurences lost interest, and the production was scrapped by Hitchcock in favor of a simpler one involving Audrey's *Green Mansions* co-star, Anthony Perkins. Though this new film, *Psycho*, became one of Hitchcock's most successful and best-remembered films, he remained resentful of Audrey for her untimely withdrawal from *No Bail for the Judge*.

Audrey was elated at the birth of her son Sean on July 17, 1960, a feeling that continued through the summer spent at Bürgenstock, Switzerland, with her mother and Sean's nanny, Gina. During this time, she was offered parts in several attractive projects, including the lead in *West Side Story* (which would go to Natalie Wood), but she preferred the rapture of her newfound maternity. "Like all mothers, I couldn't believe at first that Sean was really for me, and I could really keep him. I'm still filled with the wonder of his being, to be able to go out and come back and find that he's still there!"

However, Audrey was under contract to Paramount, and by late summer of 1960 the studio was pressuring her to get back to work. Since she had renewed her contract with Paramount in late November 1958, Audrey had been working merely as a loaner to outside studios, including Warner Bros. for *The Nun's Story*, MGM for *Green Mansions*, and United Artists for *The Unforgiven*. Furthermore, after completing *The Unforgiven*, Audrey took almost a year off around her pregnancy with Sean. Paramount, though pleased to have dodged a bullet by passing *Green Mansions* to MGM, was now eager to cash in on its valuable star.

ELLE

PEARL BUCK: "POURQUOI JE VIS"

LES LITS DE A à Z: UNE ENQUÊTE MAISON

AUDREY HEPBURN PRÉSENTE LA MODE DE PARIS

SE OG HØR

RADIO OG FJERNSYN

AUDREY i BYEN

Den yndige amerikanske skuespillerinde Audrey Hepburn
og hendes mand Mel Ferrer på besøg. Se siderne 10-11

Nr. 41. 9. oktober 1959   20. årgang.   Pris 85 øre

Page 147:
ELLE, France, October 1959

SE OG HØR, Denmark, Oct. 9, 1959

IDUN, Sweden, Oct. 4, 1959

DIN TIDNING, Denmark, September 1959

VECKO-JOURNALEN, Sweden, Oct. 2, 1959

OGGI, Italy, Jul. 28, 1960

ZONDAGSVRIEND, Netherlands, Nov. 10, 1960

SCRAPBOOK
A page from a vintage fan-made scrapbook.

SCHWEIZER ILLUSTRIERTE ZEITUNG,
Switzerland, Jan. 19, 1959

EPOCA, Italy, 1960
The international media helped the Ferrers celebrate the July 17, 1960, birth of their son, Sean Hepburn Ferrer.

TELE VIZIER

NUMMER
17 FEBR. 1962

WEEKABONNEES 40 CT
LOSSE NRS   48 CT

HET LEVEN IN BEELD
van
Audrey Hepburn

TELEVIZIER, Netherlands, Feb. 17, 1962

ZONDAGSVRIEND, Netherlands, Apr. 23, 1959

MUSIC FROM THE MOTION PICTURE SOUND-TRACK, United States, 1960
United Artists record album jacket featuring instrumental film-score by Academy Award–winning composer Dimitri Tiomkin for The Unforgiven. *The music was unusually dissonant for a western, but was appropriate for the film's complex emotional themes. The album sold poorly.*

THEME MUSIC SONG SHEET, United States, 1960
Vibrant promotional art for the sheet music cover.

TELÉRAMA, France, Oct. 16, 1960

THE SUNDAY SUN, Canada, Mar. 7, 1959
Director/producer Mel Ferrer was advised by animal trainers that in order for Audrey/Rima to bond on-screen with Pippin the fawn, the quadruped would have to be separated from its mother during infancy and become Audrey's live-in pet. Animal-lover Audrey nicknamed the fawn "Ip," and was often photographed lounging, frolicking, and even shopping with him.

CINÉ MONDE, France, Sept. 12, 1961

THIS WEEK, United States, Nov. 1, 1958

MÜNCHNER ILLUSTRIERTE, Germany, Aug. 1, 1959

BREAKFAST AT TIFFANY'S

1961–1962

AUDREY'S IMAGE THROUGHOUT THE '50S WAS AS an elfin figure: radiant, lovely, beautiful, but not what in most quarters passed for "sexy." After Sean's birth, even her theatrically high-minded husband and mentor Mel Ferrer suggested that she revisit lighter fare, but in more sophisticated and perhaps sexier roles.

Truman Capote said that while writing his novella *Breakfast at Tiffany's,* he had envisioned Marilyn Monroe as Holly Golightly, and he is reported to have sold the rights to Paramount expecting that she would star in the film. (Monroe declined, either because Twentieth Century-Fox refused to loan her services or she was advised not to reinforce her sexualized persona by playing a prostitute or both.)

Capote's original story dripped with sexuality, and was altogether more somber than the sweetened, sanitized, and diluted version provided to Paramount by screenwriter George Axelrod (who had previously worked on Monroe films such as *The Seven Year Itch* and *Bus Stop*). Capote was paid $65,000 for all rights to *Tiffany's,* so he had no say about the switch from Marilyn to Audrey, or about the transformation of his calculating and ambitious hooker with a heart of gold to a dizzy fashion princess. He later said in a 1968 *Playboy* magazine interview: "Paramount double-crossed me [in casting] Audrey. . . . The book was really rather bitter. . . . The film became a mawkish valentine to New York City and Holly and, as a result, was thin and pretty, whereas it should have been rich and ugly . . . [Audrey] is an old friend and one of my favorite people, but she was just wrong for that part."

Axelrod's Holly was a paradoxical crafty operator with high ideals, a hillbilly with an instinct for refined urban fashion, which does sound more like Norma Jean Baker/Marilyn Monroe than like Audrey Hepburn, with her blue-blood heritage and understated sexuality. Furthermore, Audrey rarely wore jewelry besides her wedding ring and diamond-studded pearl earrings. She later said, in relation to her association to Tiffany & Co. through the Holly Golightly character: "My image will never be Miss Diamonds, don't you know that?" Tiffany & Co.'s senior vice president John Loring recalled for the *People Extra* posthumous tribute issue (Winter 1993): "Anything that was flash to her was not real glamour or chic. There was no pretension." Nevertheless, her husband, her manager Kurt Frings, the director Blake Edwards (who flew to Switzerland with co-producer Martin Jurow to persuade her), and her mother all urged her to take the role.

It seems a safe bet that the participation of Monroe would have produced a film much closer to Capote's original. Instead, the film had an entirely unrelated appeal—something surprisingly timely, which would set the tone for colorful, light, comic fare for the rest of the 1960s.

Audrey rationalized her suitability for the racy role by recalling for reporters her days "starting out . . . back in London," when she "earned a bit on the side posing for pictures advertising soap and such things." She told of "the parties we girls went to, not always invited to, but always interested in the food that would be served around. If you pass by the man with the canapés more often than usual, you may get yourself a kind of meal. On the go." Audrey modestly added that she believed Holly to be "a frightened mouse who never delivered, even if she grabbed the fifty-dollar bills." In an interview with reporter and longtime friend Henry Gris, she said of the character: "Her wardrobe consisted chiefly of a single black dress, which she called her 'working outfit,' and a day dress. Had she really been a *femme legere,* she could have gotten all those minks half-promised her, and there would have been no point in her sidewalk breakfast outside Tiffany's . . ."

Once again, Edith Head was the costume supervisor for a film in which Audrey's couture was created by Hubert de Givenchy. It is a remarkable aspect of this film's legacy that it has a reputation as a fashion film, for in fact there is very little couture involved. Much of Audrey's clothing in *Tiffany's* was merely ready-mades and casual wear, including cotton and jersey pullovers, a standard trenchcoat, toreador pants and the like. Nevertheless, the few Givenchy designs made for this film created a sensation in the early '60s.

The Givenchy wardrobe for *Breakfast at Tiffany's* included a bright pink cocktail dress with matching pink low heels, bag, linen coat, and pink-tinted tiara as a whimsical novelty; a square-cut, calf-length, orange, double-breasted wool coat with kimono sleeves, a false belt terminating in a back knot, and a high upturned circular collar (accessorized with a sable cloche hat, sunglasses, and pearl earrings); and the two now legendary sleeveless "little black dresses." The short one was made of black cloqué silk, with a rounded neckline, a slightly belt-emphasized waistline, and a flared skirt edged with high ruches—accessorized by a large-brimmed hat decorated with a silk kerchief. The breathtaking longer garment, Holly's so-called "working dress" (worn by Holly in the opening scene of the film outside of Tiffany's with coffee and Danish in hand) was a satin evening gown with straight lines divided at the waist and a shaped-back neckline, accessorized with long black gloves, strands of pearls, and of course the essential tiara. Add the long cigarette holder (included for publicity shots, but not used with this outfit in the film) and the novel updo, and you have the single most celebrated image of Audrey's career.

As a side note, although a little black dress in this style is indelibly associated with Audrey, its actual pedigree dates back to 1926, when Gabrielle "Coco" Chanel created the cocktail uniform for the newly liberated and androgynous flapper. Since that time, with only slight modifications, the style remains a fashion perennial. The original creation, dubbed by American *Vogue* the "Ford of fashion," was a no-frills, straight dress in black crepe de chine, that could be adapted for any social situation. Audrey's versions from *Breakfast at Tiffany's*, both designed by Hubert de Givenchy in 1960, are among fashion's best-remembered synergies of frock and frau.

Audrey's image for the film included a peroxide-streaked, upswept twist effected by her longtime hair stylist, Grazia De Rossi. John J. O'Connell, in the *American Weekly*, June 25, 1961, reported, "What has Audrey done to her hair? Here's the scoop, straight from the set of her new movie: Hepburn switches from prim girl to playgirl in *Breakfast at Tiffany's*. Needed new hairdo to fit new character. So good-by Italian shag, hello natural brunette streaked with peroxide blonde, up-swept for nightlife scenes. Jazzy? Jazzy, indeed. Miss Hepburn likes it, too, now wears it this way off the screen as well."

The success of *Breakfast at Tiffany's* reestablished Audrey's screen career, transforming her from bright-eyed ingénue, harbinger and promulgator of the youthful styles of the '50s, to sophisticated trendsetter of the '60s. Never mind that she was dreadfully miscast in the role of Holly Golightly, the vehicle of her image transformation. It seems that Audrey's celebrity never completely relied on the popularity of her films or even her versatility as an actress, though in both arenas she scored her share of triumphs.

LIFE

INTERNATIONAL

JAPAN'S TROUBLES

WITH NEUTRALISM

SUPERSONIC TRAVEL

London-New York
In 132 Minutes

AUDREY
HEPBURN

In Her
Funniest Role

M$N25	DOMINICAN REP.	20c	GUATEMALA	20c	JORDAN	120 Fils	NEW ZEALAND	2 -	SPAIN & POSS.	Pts 17
2 6	EAST AFRICA	2 -	HAITI	G 1.00	KOREA	Hwan 325	NICARAGUA	C$1,50	SURINAM	60c
S 7	ECUADOR	S 4	HONDURAS	40c	KUWAIT	120 Fils	NIGERIA	2 -	SWEDEN	KR 1.60 inkl oms
Fr 14	EGYPT	Pi 15	HONG KONG	HK$2.00	LAOS	K 25	NORWAY	Kr 2	SWITZERLAND	Fr 1.20

LIFE INTERNATIONAL, Netherlands, Oct. 9, 1961
A stunning cover for Life's *international edition.*

LECTURAS, Spain, June 29, 1962

CINELÂNDIA, Brazil, December 1961

EIGA NO TOMO, Japan, January 1961
These pages from Japanese Screen Story *magazine showcases Givenchy's square-cut, calf length, orange double breasted coat in double wool, featuring kimono sleeves and upturned, circular collar.*

EPOCA, Italy, Oct. 15, 1961

SEDUÇÃO, Brazil, 1962

BILD JOURNALEN, Sweden, Jan. 17, 1962
Spectacular double front-cover issue of Swedish Bild *devoted to the two stars of* Breakfast At Tiffany's.

FILM NEUES, Germany, January 1962

OUR WORLD, Israel, Apr. 27, 1962

VEA Y LEA, Spain, Aug. 3, 1961
A rarely used publicity shot from Breakfast At Tiffany's.

JOURS DE FRANCE, France, Jan. 27, 1962

JOURS DE FRANCE

Audrey
Hepburn
l'actrice
la plus
élégante
du
monde

N° 376 - 1 NF
27 JANV. 1962

168

FILME, Spain, August 1961

CINE NOVELAS, Mexico, March 1962

MOTION PICTURE SCORE, United States, 1961
RCA 7" 45 rpm record sleeve of composer Henry Mancini's instrumental versions of Moon River *and* Breakfast at Tiffany's

SCREEN, Japan, October 1962
BOLERO FILM, Italy, Mar. 18, 1962

キネマ旬報

2

決算特別号

★ 1962年度封切映画総覧
★ ショウ・ビジネス昨年の決算

MOTION PICTURE TIMES

MOTION PICTURE TIMES, Japan, Feb. 1, 1963

THE AMERICAN WEEKLY, United States, Jun. 25, 1961

LIBERTY, Canada, March 1963

QUICK, Germany, November 1961

PANORAMA CHRÉTIEN, France, September 1962

EIGA STORY, Japan, December 1961

TV MAGAZINE, United States, Apr. 6, 1962

FILM EN TELEVISIE, Belgium, March 1962

OUR WORLD, Israel, Feb. 22, 1962

CINÉMA 62, France, February 1962

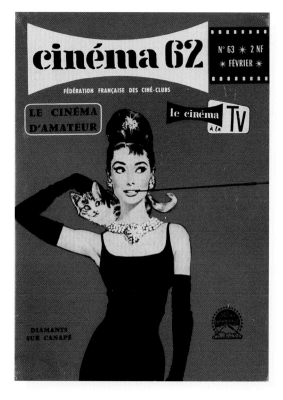

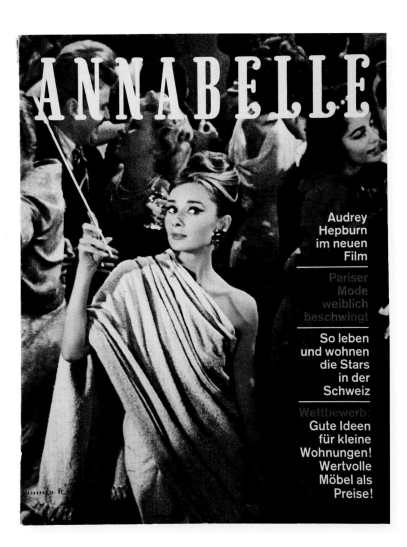

ANNABELLE, Germany, February 1962
PANTHEON, Greece, 1962
L'EUROPEO, Italy, Dec. 10, 1961

LOBBY CARD, United States, 1961
Commercial artist Robert McGinnis's famous image of Audrey adorned the posters and theater lobby cards for Breakfast at Tiffany's. This example, number six of eight, is generally regarded as the most outstanding of the American theater lobby card set.

LIFE INTERNATIONAL, Netherlands, Oct. 9, 1961
Interior spread from the magazine.

PARAMOUNT WORLD, United States, July 1961
Paramount Studios industry journal Paramount World featuring Audrey in one of the two now-legendary little black dresses used in the film.

THE CHILDREN'S HOUR,

1962–1964

CHARADE *and* PARIS WHEN IT SIZZLES

KURT FRINGS, AUDREY'S HIGH-POWERED MANAGER beginning in 1954, had a reputation as a shrewd negotiator who scored lucrative contracts for his mostly female clients—including Elizabeth Taylor, Brigitte Bardot, Lucille Ball, and Olivia de Havilland—and he was used to his clients valuing his insights into their careers. He understood Audrey's unique charisma, and made substantive decisions on her behalf. (Audrey was certainly one of his most lucrative clients.) But he was also frustrated by Audrey's dodging of his career advancing recommendations in favor of her own domestic priorities. With an eye on landing her money- and reputation-making roles in musicals and blockbusters, Frings had already drawn many major offers that Audrey had turned down, including the musicals *Gigi* and *West Side Story*—two of the top grossing musicals of all time—as well as the starring role in *Cleopatra*, whose record-breaking salary for a leading lady went to Elizabeth Taylor. It became abundantly clear that Audrey's aspiration was to work only when it fit around the ranking priorities of her home and family life.

A dedicated and hard-working actress, Audrey was not passionate about career in and of itself, and she increasingly wanted to work only in films shot either near her home in Switzerland (Rome or Paris being acceptably close) or shot soon enough after a preceding project that she wouldn't have to move her son, his nanny, and all her traveling accommodations into a new hotel, bungalow, or temporary house. Some significant opportunities evaporated when Hollywood producers willing to pay her daunting salary could not also move entire productions nearer her European home.

Audrey told journalist Mary Worthington Jones in *Photoplay* some years earlier, "Mel and I both value our careers immensely. We'd be very foolish and irresponsible if we didn't. [But] if we ever said, 'Oh, just this once, what does it matter if we separated for a few short months,' then the once becomes twice—without realizing it, we might have let material success ruin two lives. . . . If I were asked to take a step which might jeopardize my marriage, I would delve deep down into my heart to discover *why* I must do this."

At thirty, Audrey would have been just as happy to retire after *The Unforgiven*, raising Sean and quietly withdrawing into the humble role of Mrs. Mel Ferrer, Swiss housewife and mother. But Ferrer was ambitious for both their careers. Reportedly, after 1960, it was in response to his urging that Audrey accepted assignments that took her away from domesticity.

By the early '60s, Audrey had cloistered herself away from the Hollywood scene, which limited her promotional opportunities and interviews. Most interviews were done only with pre-approved scripts, and this contributed to the perception that Audrey was treated as royalty when she was in Hollywood.

In 1962, having completed her six-picture contract with Paramount, Audrey reinforced her detachment from conventional Hollywood protocols by emerging as one of the first unffiliated independents negotiating entirely on her own terms. This gave her the liberty to accept and reject assignments with even more autonomy. Except for her role in *My Fair Lady* in 1964, which Frings negotiated with all his considerable skill, the art and legacy of Audrey's roles through the rest of the 1960s, starting with *The Children's Hour* in 1962, are increasingly erratic.

With fortunate timing for him, director William Wyler

proposed a remake of Lillian Hellman's controversial *The Children's Hour* just as Audrey was wrapping *Breakfast at Tiffany's* in Hollywood, and though she was eager to return to the duties of motherhood, she also felt obliged to work with the director who had helped launch her career with *Roman Holiday*. Conveniently, she and her family were already temporarily ensconced in Hollywood.

The original 1934 play *The Children's Hour* was based on a nineteenth-century Scottish court case. It is a drama about two matrons at a private girls' school whose lives are destroyed by a child's malicious lie about their alleged homosexual involvement. Despite critical and commercial success on Broadway, the play was passed over for the Pulitzer Prize, resulting in historic outrage in the New York press and the founding of the annual New York Drama Critics' Circle Award.

Wyler had filmed a bowdlerized, Production Code–compromised adaptation of the play in 1936 under the title *These Three*. He still trusted in the plot's enduring themes, and by the 1960s interpreted the changed times as an opportunity to produce an undiluted version. However, even in 1960, the film's producers insisted on a less bleak ending than the original, and after several options were considered, a compromise was reached in which the demise of Martha Dobie (Shirley MacLaine) was offset by more hopeful aftermaths for the lovers Karen Wright (Audrey Hepburn) and Dr. Joe Cardin (James Garner).

It would be nice to think that Audrey had accepted roles in *The Unforgiven* and *The Children's Hour* with an eye to social justice, but she seems to have taken the roles based on other considerations, and was reportedly unnerved by the lesbian allusions in the latter story. Frederick Raphael, screenwriter for Audrey's 1967 film *Two for the Road*, recalled that when he sent his screenplay *Richard's Things* to her in the late 1970s, Audrey returned it saying that she "couldn't begin to think of playing the role of a woman that falls in love with another woman," and that she had once played such a role in *The Children's Hour*, and it had proved so unrewarding in every sense except the most literal that she had put the experience completely out of her mind.

After completing *The Children's Hour*, Audrey made two more films back to back, both shot in Paris, *Paris When It Sizzles* (filmed in 1962, but not released until 1964) and *Charade* (1963). Both projects were contemporary films set in Europe, and no imperative in either plot line suggested the heroine need be anything but *tres chic*. Audrey's modern European couture in both productions would naturally be designed by Hubert de Givenchy.

Paris When It Sizzles SOUNDED QUITE PROMISING; the screenplay was written by George Axelrod, screenwriter for *Breakfast at Tiffany's*, and the film reunited Audrey with her *Sabrina* costar William Holden. Cameo appearances included Marlene Dietrich, Tony Curtis, and even Mel Ferrer. The concept was based on a 1952 French film, *La Fête à Henriette* (*Holiday for Henrietta*), written and directed by Julien Duvivier. Axelrod's screenplay casts Holden as Richard Benson, a playboy screenwriter with two days until deadline for a script called *The Girl Who Stole the Eiffel Tower*. Naturally, Benson has been drinking and partying in the preceding months. In the last days remaining before the deadline,

Benson hires Gabrielle Simpson (Audrey) as a temporary secretary to spend the weekend in the apartment and help as stenographer. They proceed to invent scenarios frantically for the screenplay by acting them out in a series of fantasy sequences.

For the movie, Givenchy is credited not only with Audrey's wardrobe (restrained by Givenchy standards), but also her perfume. Perhaps the most acid evaluation came from a critic who remarked that "the perfume couldn't be smelled but the picture could." The light, kidding style of the film was almost universally interpreted as simply bad acting and direction.

Perhaps the best thing about the film was that it inspired a chorus of snide, witty reviews, including Judith Crist's jabs in the *New York Herald Tribune*, "Miss Hepburn is, as always, very lovely to look at, and so is Paris. Mr. Holden, however, is not Cary Grant, even though he tries and he tries and he tries. And *Paris When It Sizzles*? Strictly Hollywood when-it-fizzles." Stanley Kauffman of the *New Republic* added, "Contributions are in order from admirers of Audrey Hepburn to buy and suppress all copies of *Paris When It Sizzles*. It is based on an old Duvivier opus, which itself was deadly; the new script by George Axelrod embalms the original instead of reviving it. His dialogue and Holden's gift for comedy amply deserve each other. And in the midst of this meager harvest is Miss Audrey Hepburn trying to make chaff out of corn."

Much to Audrey's chagrin, *Paris When It Sizzles* wrapped late due to constant delays (including a week's hiatus mid-shoot to allow alcoholic costar Holden to dry out). With only a single day's rest after finalizing Paris, *Charade* began production.

Audrey was glad for the opportunity to finally work with the elusive Cary Grant, who had turned down the parts of Linus Larrabee in *Sabrina* and playboy Frank Flannagan in *Love in the Afternoon*. In both cases, Grant realistically believed the twenty-five-year age difference would be awkward in an on-screen romance. Screenwriter Peter Stone assured Grant that although there would be a romantic tug between his character, Peter Joshua, and Audrey's Reggie Lambert, he would not be presented in romantic pursuit of the younger woman.

Charade was envisioned in the mold of Alfred Hitchcock's trademark thrillers, but was sadly lacking their wit, psychological interest, and obsessive attention to detail. The film begins with the cliché of an unnamed man being thrown off a train in France. Minutes later, the action switches to the ultra-chic Audrey sporting oversized sunglasses and a Givenchy ski suit on the terrace of a posh ski lodge at Megève, Switzerland. There she is met by an impeccably tailored Cary Grant, but not before being slowly approached by someone creeping off-screen with a drawn gun. That the gun proves to be a squirt gun in the hands of a small boy demonstrates the film's disappointing flippancy. Once back in Paris, Audrey discovers that her apartment has been emptied to the walls and her husband is missing (it was he who was thrown off the train), and Grant volunteers to help her solve the mystery of her husband's disappearance. The only real suspense comes in what new Givenchy creation will be unveiled in each scene. Andrew Sarris of the *Village Voice* characterized the film as displaying "the sick elegance of a fashion show in a funeral parlor . . . With a plot that smells of red herrings . . ."

The couture of both *Paris When It Sizzles* and *Charade* is in some ways traditional Givenchy, showcasing his hallmark of reserve and finish. The fashions are stylish, but are less obviously intent on innovation than those in *Funny Face* or *Breakfast at Tiffany's*. The looks instead carry the toned-down inflection of Oleg Cassini, the talented but often derivative couturier to newly established fashion icon, First Lady Jacqueline Kennedy. Cassini's simplified interpretations of French design's by Karl Lagerfeld, Federico Forquet, Coco Chanel and, significantly, Givenchy, were made affordable and available to a large group of American women, and this availability created a mainstream fashion taste the economics of which inevitably affected the course of French couture. The shift in fashion tastes brought about by Cassini diminished Audrey's role as a totem of contemporary fashion, and also displaced Paris as the center of the world fashion scene. The '60s saw the rise of ready-to-wear clothes, attention turned to London, Scandinavia, and New York, and trends were set by stylish youth or youth-oriented designers, such as André Courrèges and Mary Quant.

Audrey's archetypal fashion influence and cutting edge currency had been an effect, but not the goal of her costuming choices, and her continuing preference of Givenchy creations for both *Paris When It Sizzles* and *Charade* demonstrates an uncompromising, more personal style. She wore what was right for her, and her increasing indifference to trends, even those she had helped establish, amplified her iconic power.

DE POST, Netherlands, August 1962

ROTOSEI SETTIMANALE, Italy, Jan. 8, 1962

ECRAN, Chile, Mar. 16, 1962

ELLE, France, 1962

LIFE, United States, Apr. 20, 1962

LIFE

THE GLORY AND BEAUTY OF ROME

APRIL 20 · 1962 · 20¢

MOVIE NEWS, United States, July 1962
After Breakfast At Tiffany's*, Audrey's face and look had become icons of beauty and style regardless of her current cinematic vehicle. In 1962 and 1963, magazine coverage would frequently include a fetching cover portrait without connection to any article within the magazine.*

CINE UNIVERSAL, Mexico, Jun. 15, 1962

SES, Turkey, Apr. 11, 1964

LE FILM ILLUSTRÉ, France, 1962

MOVIELAND AND TV TIME, United States, June 1962

VANIDADES, United States, Jul. 1, 1962

EIGA NO TOMO, Japan, May 1962

BRAVO, Germany, Aug. 31, 1963

FILMSKI SVET, Poland, 1963

NEDERLANDS FAMILIEBLAD REVUE,
Netherlands, Sept. 28, 1963

AMIS DU FILM, Belgium, March 1964

STRIP, Netherlands, Nov. 10, 1962
SCREEN, Japan, May 1963
FRIMOUSSE, France, 1962

ELOKUVA-AITTA, Finland, 1962

ZONDAGSVRIEND, Germany, Jun. 21, 1962

FRANKFURTER ILLUSTRIERTE, Germany, Jun. 24, 1962

PARIS MATCH, France, Jul. 8, 1961

OUR WORLD, Israel, Sept. 6, 1962

FILM REVUE, Germany, Jun. 19, 1962
At thirty-three, Audrey's face had finally lost its adolescence and begun to embody a more mature, feminine beauty.

SES, Turkey, Oct. 23, 1965

ROSITA, Netherlands, Apr. 25, 1964

WOMAN'S DAY, Australia, Oct. 28, 1963

SPECTATOR Greece, 1962

JOURS DE FRANCE, France, Jun. 30, 1962

BRIGITTE, Germany, January 1963

Brigitte

C 1940 D

Audrey
Hepburn:
„Meine
drei Männer"

Grosses
Silvester-Orakel:
Das bringt Ihnen
as neue Jahr!

1 80 Pfennig
Januar 1963

SCREEN, Japan, October 1962

CHARADE PROGRAM, Japan, 1963
Audrey in Givenchy on location at Mont d'Arbois resort in Megeve, Switzerland, for the opening scene of Charade.

CHARADE PROGRAM, Japan, 1963
This smart Givenchy skiing outfit was mostly covered by the fur poncho and turban of Charade's *opening scene. The 1963 Japanese theatrical program ran this striking gatefold display of the costume elements that were not visible in the film.*

SEURA, Finland, Apr. 30, 1963

VECKO REVYN, Sweden, Apr. 4, 1963

STERN, Germany, Feb. 10, 1963

ECRAN, Chile, Dec. 20, 1963

BOLERO FILM, Italy, Apr. 28, 1963

シャレード

PROGRAM, Japan, 1963
Japanese theatrical program for Charade.

PROGRAM, Japan, 1963
Because of his actual age difference with Audrey, Cary Grant's Charade *contract stipulated that the characters be rewritten so that his was not to be romantically pursuing hers. However, vice versa was OK.*

SIZ, Turkey, Feb. 7, 1966

LOOK, United States, Dec. 17, 1963
Cary and Audrey were very particular about the publicity images circulated for this film, each rejecting images the other might have approved because only one was looking their best. Rumor has it that in the case of unresolved conflict, Audrey's choice prevailed.

LOOK

NOW MORE THAN 7,400,000 CIRCULATION

25 CENTS · DECEMBER 17, 1963

PREVIEW POLL:
KENNEDY
COULD LOSE

THE NEGRO
FACES
NORTH

CARY
GRANT
THE LEGEND & THE LADIES

AUDREY
HEPBURN
LEADING LADY No. 50

REVUE

**Audrey Hepburn
leest hier een
Revue
waar zij zelf
op staat**

REVUE *het nederlands familieblad*

Audrey Hepburn

Voor abonnees 35 ct.
Losse nummers 45 ct.
Verschijnt wekelijks

REVUE, Netherlands, Mar. 3, 1962

AJAN SÄVEL, Finland, November 1962
With millinery poised to go the way of whalebone and bustles by the early 1960s, Audrey lends her chic to an ailing industry by modeling in diverse chapeaus.

NOVA ANTENA, Portugal, Feb. 14, 1969

SCREEN, Japan, 1963

FILMS IN REVIEW, United States, 1964
Exotic costumes from a fantasy sequence in Paris When It Sizzles.

MY FAIR LADY

1964–
1965

THE ROLE OF ELIZA DOOLITTLE WAS PERHAPS the most coveted in Hollywood since Scarlett O'Hara in *Gone With the Wind*. The 1956 stage musical was based on George Bernard Shaw's play *Pygmalion*, which Shaw himself had adapted for a successful British film production in 1938. By Shaw's death in 1950, the songwriting team of Alan Jay Lerner and Frederick Loewe (*Brigadoon, Paint Your Wagon, Gigi,* and *Camelot*) had already scored the play to music and lyrics, and they quickly secured rights to the play. It would be filmed as *My Fair Lady*, and the plan was to cast Rex Harrison as the misogynistic professor of phonetics Henry Higgins and (after Mary Martin declined) feature Julie Andrews as Eliza Doolittle, the unkempt cockney flower girl who would be passed off as a duchess at the Embassy Ball. The flower girl turned lady succeeds at the ball, takes umbrage at Higgins's treatment of her, and departs, leaving Higgins to realize that he has fallen in love with her. Although Shaw had intended the play as Edwardian social protest, audiences enjoy it today as a romantic Cinderella story.

The film was almost certain to be a blockbuster. The Broadway production of *My Fair Lady* had won the Outer Circle, Tony, and New York Drama Critics' Circle awards; it was at the time the longest-running show ever in New York and London, and would be produced in more than twenty countries; the original cast album sold more than five million copies. Warner Bros. paid Lerner and Loewe more than $5 million for the license and marshaled director George Cukor and choreographer Hermes Pan to insure their investment.

Rex Harrison was not Jack Warner's first choice, but once he was set on Rex Harrison bringing his Higgins from stage to film, he was doubtful that virtually unknown Andrews was right for Eliza Doolittle. Audrey, who had made the unlikely *Nun's Story* one of Warner Bros.'s biggest-grossing films to date, was the first choice. Warner felt that the only way to guarantee his investment in the screenplay was to hire the only actress with a guaranteed following, and he knew that that actress was Audrey Hepburn. Through Kurt Frings's hard-nosed negotiation, Audrey would take home a million dollars plus a percentage of the gross.

Warner's passing over of Andrews, who had played the role on Broadway, reflected badly on Audrey. Many movie fans and industry players thought she had stolen the role that should have gone to Andrews, and Loewe from that point on reportedly resented the entire project and rarely visited the set. *My Fair Lady* all but swept the Academy Awards in 1965, but without even a nomination for Audrey as best actress (the award went to Andrews for her role in *Mary Poppins*). Upon hearing that Audrey had not garnered a nomination, Katharine Hepburn (no relation) thoughtfully sent a telegram that said: "Don't worry about not being nominated. Some day you'll get another one for a part that doesn't rate."

Audrey undertook up to twelve hours per day of rehearsals for the role of Eliza, including singing lessons under Susan Seton, rehearsals and recordings with arranger André Previn and musical director Ray Heindorf, Cockney lessons with professor Peter Ladefoged, and dance rehearsals with Hermes Pan. Harrison had prerecorded his singing parts, but by the time shooting began in August of 1963, Audrey was still struggling. She finished the soundtrack recordings, but Lerner and Loewe decided in the end to overdub Marni Nixon's voice for both film and soundtrack LP release. (Nixon had previously provided vocal dubbing for Deborah Kerr in *The King and I* and Natalie Wood in *West Side Story*.) It fell to Heindorf to inform Audrey of the decision. Learning that her months of singing practice and her recording sessions had been wasted and that every note of her songs would be replaced, she reportedly fled the soundstage in disappointment. Returning the following day, she apologized to her fellow cast members. Worse still, this unfortunate turn of events furthered the misperception that Audrey, who couldn't sing the part, had been given it unfairly over Andrews.

Audrey would later say that Eliza Doolittle was her most difficult role in that, unlike her previous roles, she didn't see any part of herself in the character. Biographically, some might be tempted to see in the Svengali Henry Higgins a bit of her husband Ferrer, but this was not how Audrey saw herself or the role.

The period costume design, by Cecil Beaton, was modeled on Shaw's Edwardian England circa 1910. Audrey said of Beaton's work, "No one had so extensive a knowledge of the time in which *My Fair Lady* is set as he. He was familiar with all the nuances of fashion of the time, and that is why his costumes for the film were of such unsurpassable elegance. I shall never forget the endlessly long wardrobe rooms at Paramount for that film, packed with all sorts of accessories—feathers, flowers, lace, tulle, coats, hats, and shoes, as far as one could see. Cecil Beaton had accumulated most of this treasure trove from museums, private houses, and secondhand shops."

Lyricist Alan Jay Lerner said of Beaton, "When you looked at him, it was difficult to know whether he designed the Edwardian era or the Edwardian era designed him."

Beaton arrived in Hollywood in February 1963 to start work on the one thousand meticulously detailed costumes called for in his plans. Each of the four hundred black and white gowns for the Ascot Gavotte scene alone would be recreated from museum sources and attended to with the detailing usually reserved for the costuming of principal cast members.

As a period film, *My Fair Lady* did not much influence contemporary fashion—no bustles and whalebone corsets for the liberated, feminist '60s. The ultra-feminizing fashions did, however, showcase Audrey's beauty. While it featured none of Audrey's personal chic, its Cinderella theme (variations of which figured in *Roman Holiday, Sabrina,* and *Funny Face*) is the cornerstone of the Hepburn image. And the fashions, while not her "style," established her as a symbol of natural, elegant beauty—a consummate feminine muse—the ideal postmodern woman. Director George Cukor (known for expert direction of women, including Greta Garbo, Katharine Hepburn, Joan Crawford, Lauren Bacall, Claudette Colbert, Marlene Dietrich, and Vivien Leigh) quipped of Audrey, "She's the fairest lady of them all."

Writer Peer J. Oppenheimer observed in *Family Weekly* (March 1964), "[Audrey's career] has made her the second highest-paid actress in the world (Elizabeth Taylor is first). Liz's appeal is easy to account for, but Audrey's is not so apparent. Could it be that, even in this age, the average woman yearns to be a 'fair lady'—and that the average man has an unfashionable, but unquenchable, admiration for such supposedly outdated beauty?"

ΕΙΚΟΝΕΣ

ΑΡ. 500 · 21 ΜΑΪΟΥ 1965 · ΔΡ. 5

ΤΟ ΡΑΛΛΥ ΑΝΤΙΚΑ

ΜΙΑ ΜΕΓΑΛΗ ΕΠΙΤΥΧΙΑ
ΠΟΥ ΓΙΝΕΤΑΙ ΘΕΣΜΟΣ

Ή τραγωδία στὸ Λευκοχώρι

ΡΕΠΟΡΤΑΖ
ΤΟΥ κ. Θ. ΔΑΣΚΑΛΟΠΟΥΛΟΥ

ΩΝΤΡΕΫ ΧΕΠΜΠΟΡΝ

PICTURES, Greece, May 1965

FAMILY WEEKLY, United States, Mar. 8, 1964

REVUE, Netherlands, Dec. 4, 1965

COLORATO MAGAZINE, United States, Nov. 1, 1964
An uncommon publicity portrait for My Fair Lady sans Cecil Beaton period costuming. This weekend tabloid newspaper insert magazine was issued shortly after the Oct. 21, 1964, New York premiere.

LADIES HOME COMPANION, United States, September 1964
The spectacular Cecil Beaton gown for the Ascot Gavotte scene in My Fair Lady.

SCHWEIZER ILLUSTRIERTE ZEITUNG, Switzerland, Dec. 28, 1964

BUNTE ILLUSTRIERTE, Germany, Jan. 13, 1964

STERN, Germany, July 26, 1964

LE PATRIOTE ILLUSTRÉ, France, Sept. 13, 1964

WEEKEND MAGAZINE, Canada, Aug. 22, 1964

**MY FAIR LADY
GOES TO HOLLYWOOD**

see page 10

Victoria Daily Times | weekenD Magazine

VOL. 14, No. 34   AUG. 22, 1964

CECIL BEATON'S FAIR LADY, England, 1964
Cecil Beaton's 1964 diary/memoir of his experiences designing sets and costumes for My Fair Lady. *The original British dust jacket is pictured here.*

MARIE CLAIRE, France, Mar. 15, 1964

PROGRAM, Japan, 1964
Japanese theatrical program for My Fair Lady.

FILM IDEAL, Spain, Jun. 15, 1964

LA FAMILIA, Mexico, Feb. 15, 1965

PROGRAM, France, 1964
French theatrical program for My Fair Lady.

LA NOTICIA CON OJOS DE MUJER, Argentina,
Mar. 13, 1965

ANDRÉ PREVIN AND HIS ORCHESTRA ALBUM,
United States, 1964
*Columbia Records LP featuring My Fair Lady musical
arranger André Previn's jazz interpretation of the score.*

MUNDO URUGUAYO, Uruguay, Sept. 23, 1964

MY FAIR LADY, Sweden, 1967
*Attractive Swedish hardbound pictorial novelization of My
Fair Lady.*

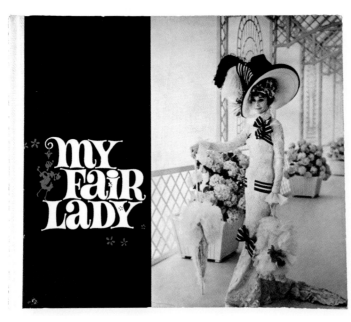

DAMERNAS VÄRLD, Sweden, Aug. 12, 1964

SCREEN STORIES, United States, December 1964

SOUND STAGE, United States, December 1964

STERN WIENER ILLUSTRIERTE, Austria, Apr. 5, 1964

FAIR LADY, United States, Fall 1964

Америка

№ 109/Цена 50 к

ОДРИ ХЕПБЭРН В ФИЛЬМЕ

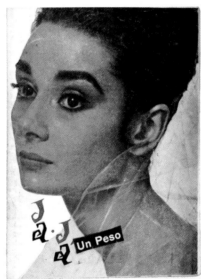

AMERICA, Russia, 1964

LADIES HOME JOURNAL, February 1964

VOGUE, France, May 1963

VOGUE, United States, November 1964

JA JA, Mexico, Nov. 5, 1964

WOMAN'S JOURNAL, England, February 1965

JOURS
DE
FRANCE

AUDREY
HEPBURN

N° 613 - 1,20 F - 13 AOUT 1966

CE NUMÉRO A ÉTÉ TIRÉ À 1 MILLION D'EXEMPLAIRES

JOURS DE FRANCE, France, Aug. 13, 1966

LADIES' HOME JOURNAL, September 1963

TODAY'S CHARM, United States, Fall 1964

ELLE, France, Jan. 10, 1964

FILMSKI SVET, Poland, Oct. 22, 1964

DUGA, Poland, Jan. 23, 1966

SCREEN, Japan, January 1965
Below and bottom left and right: cover and interior pages.

SCREEN, Japan, March 1965

COSMOPOLITAN, United States, March 1964
The juxtaposition on these interior pages suggest Audrey's ostracism for having been chosen to portray Warner Brothers' cinematic Eliza Dolittle, unseating Julie Andrews, popular creator of the Broadway role.

EIGA NO TOMO, Japan, February 1965

COSMOPOLITAN, United States, March 1964

BASTEI STELLA-ROMAN, Germany, January 1968

Hollywood's New Fair Lady

The Lerner-Loewe musical which starred Julie Andrews as the Fair Lady of Broadway for 1,296 performances has grossed more than $100,000,000. Now Hollywood is gambling $17,000,000 on a new Eliza Doolittle: Audrey Hepburn.

BY JOHN KEATING

In George Bernard Shaw's comedy, *Pygmalion,* an iconoclastic professor of phonetics named Henry Higgins transforms Eliza Doolittle, a "draggle-tailed guttersnipe" of a cockney flower seller, into a "lady" and passes her off at an elegant embassy ball. Higgins discovers that he has created not just a proper-speaking puppet, but, like the Pygmalion of ancient Greek legend, has brought into being a person with a soul and mind of her own. One of Shaw's most popular plays, it was turned into the most successful musical comedy in history by Lerner and Loewe.

The original production of *My Fair Lady* ran on Broadway for six and a half years, its 2,717 performances breaking all long-run records for a musical while taking in an unprecedented $20,220,000 at the box office.

The road company did even better. Crisscrossing the Continent several times and jumping to Russia for about eight weeks in 1960, the roadsters grossed some $21,500,000 in the six years and eight months between their opening performance in March, 1957, and their finale last December. It was, of course, the longest consecutive road tour in theatrical history. The English company played for 2,281 performances at the Theatre Royal, Drury Lane, London's oldest present-day theater still standing on its original site, and attracted the largest gross—$9,996,000—in the house's three-hundred-year history.

Not even Columbia Broadcasting Sys-
(continued)

DARLINGS of Broadway audiences were Julie Andrews, Rex Harrison. For Julie it was start of US stardom.

WISH COME TRUE. Three years ago Audrey Hepburn said that she'd give anything to play Eliza.

BASTEI
Stella-Roman

Das Glück, von dir geliebt zu werden

Warum ein Frauenherz immer wieder verzeiht · Von Blanca-Maria

COSMOPOLITAN

MARCH 1964

PRINCESS GRACE
A Candid Account by Her Lady-in-Waiting

Why the Wealthy Live by the Stars

NORTH SHORE WOMEN
*Massachusetts Bay
Long Island Sound
Lake Michigan*

A New Fair Lady
The Timeless Appeal of Professor Higgins' Little Flower Girl

COMPLETE MYSTERY NOVEL

映画の友

SPECIAL ISSUE
EIGA NO TOMO

AUDREY HEPBURN

HOW TO STEAL A MILLION

1966–1967

and TWO FOR THE ROAD

FOR ADMIRERS OF AUDREY HEPBURN, THE LOVE affair never ends, but fashion's judgment is less sentimental. After *My Fair Lady,* contemporary fashions returned in Audrey's next two films; but her style-icon status was increasingly eclipsed by a younger generation of actresses unlikely to be taking cues from Audrey, such as Julie Christie and Jane Fonda. In any case, Audrey preferred to camp in the kitchen making sandwiches for her preschool son rather than embody the fashion zeitgeist.

After the heartbreaks of making *My Fair Lady,* Audrey took most of 1965 off. Ferrer, in hopes of patching up their ailing marriage, suggested revisiting two projects that they had discussed working on together: an adaptation of J. M. Barrie's *Peter Pan* and a film based on the story of Empress Josephine, the wife of Napoleon. Neither would materialize, because Disney held the rights to *Peter Pan* and financial backers were reluctant to invest in the Josephine project.

Nevertheless, poised to put her hat back in the ring, Audrey accepted a project called *Venus Rising,* eventually released as *How to Steal a Million,* which was to be her third and final film under the direction of William Wyler. The plot of Harry Kurnitz's screenplay concerns the daughter (Audrey) of a third-generation art forger (Hugh Griffith), who makes the mistake of lending his family's reproduction of Cellini's *Venus* to a Paris art museum. When the family discovers that the museum plans to have the object appraised for insurance purposes, they decide to steal the statue, and a comic caper ensues. The "society burglar" hired to abscond with the bust turns out to be a detective (Peter O'Toole, refreshingly three years Audrey's junior) who had been on the forger's trail. All ends well in slapstick and matrimony.

Once again, Audrey was filming in Paris, with Wyler, and costumed by Givenchy. As an anonymous reviewer in the *Monthly Film Bulletin* noted, Audrey gave "her usual warm impersonation of wide-eyed, guileful innocence." *Newsweek* added that Audrey, "dressed to the nines by Givenchy, bejeweled by Cartier [and] terribly chic . . . [seemed to be] trading rather too heavily on her usual selection of charm." Unfortunately, the film's fashion elements came off as too staged, showcasing Audrey as a star, rather than in character.

The first sight of Audrey is in a Givenchy suit and hat with huge, bug-eye sunglasses, typical of a look one critic complained was "so extremely stylish it is virtually repellent." In a scene where Audrey gets up from reading in bed in the middle of the night to find O'Toole burglarizing her living room, she confronts the situation with a salon-teased beehive and eyes done to perfection. The fashion becomes a subject of meta-dialogue when Audrey is disguised by O'Toole in a cleaning woman's shabby dress. He says, "That does it!" "Does what?" she asks. "Well, for one thing, it gives Givenchy a night off."

In this film, Audrey's style seems for the first time to be following rather than setting trends or existing independent of them. It was stylish, but for the first time in a contemporary-set film, the style didn't seem to be hers.

Style had changed significantly in just the two years since *Charade.* The emerging taste for pop and camp, typified by Andy Warhol's art and André Courrèges's couture, was in neither Audrey's nor Givenchy's comfort zone. Why she strayed this once from her own generally impeccable and sometimes even revolutionary taste is hinted at somewhere between two contradictory statements Audrey made nearly ten years apart. In 1955, she said to a French journalist, "Why change? Everyone has his own style. When you have found it, and this is difficult, you should stick to it." In 1966, she told the *Ladies' Home Journal,* "All convention is rigidifying, I think we should try to avoid being rigid—that does age one."

DIRECTOR STANLEY DONEN SENT AUDREY AN early draft of Frederic Raphael's script for *Two for the Road,* which involved abrupt flashback sequences. She declined, citing an unnamed previous film (undoubtedly *Paris When It Sizzles*) that had also used edited vignettes, but to unsatisfying effect. Donen was so convinced that the part was right for her that, months later, he and Raphael flew to Switzerland to personally deliver the final screenplay and ask Audrey to reconsider. She said she loved this final version, and despite misgivings having to do with its "modernness," she would do it. "Audrey usually makes up her own mind about what she's going to do," Mel Ferrer told *The Ladies' Home Journal* in 1966. "This time I read the script through, and told her to take it right away. I knew it would be good for her."

Two for the Road is set almost entirely outdoors in sunny locales throughout France. The marriage appears to be headed for the rocks, but flashbacks demonstrate both cause for present misery and hopefulness. The film's deliberately trivial dialogue and frequent humor gather real emotional momentum and intensity through the flashbacks.

The plot calls for great versatility. Audrey plays a teenager, and later is found frolicking at Riviera beaches, frugging in discotheques, falling into swimming pools, having sex in hotel rooms with both characters dabbling in adultery. The film incarnated a new Audrey, sexier, earthier, and more emotionally sophisticated than any of her previous roles. Although Audrey's role in *Two for the Road* has little of the glamour and romantic fantasy for which she is best remembered, it's generally considered her best dramatic role, and one with which she could identify—the story of twelve years of a difficult marriage that is coming to an end. It was made while Audrey was coming to grips with the end of her own twelve-year marriage to Mel Ferrer. This would be Audrey's last great project as a star, and her admirers are fortunate that constellations and advisors aligned to bring it into fruition despite her many reservations about making changes to her on-screen image.

In an image change of another sort, Donen refused to allow Givenchy to design Audrey's wardrobe, saying that the wife of an architect would be unlikely to be able to afford original couture. The director was also being advised that the Givenchy style was outdated, and that the fastidious cut of his clothing clashed with the informal modern look that the writer and director were visualizing. Audrey disagreed, and was quoted as saying "Hubert [de Givenchy] makes me feel so sure of myself. I'll give a better performance in his clothes." Donen made an accommodating gesture by visiting Givenchy's Paris showrooms with Audrey and Ferrer, only to say, "Smashing. But wrong. We will find your wardrobe in boutiques."

The wardrobe in *Two for the Road* ended up to be a radical departure from the customary Givenchy-and-white-glove chic Audrey wore in *Charade* and *How to Steal a Million.* Instead, Audrey was presented in a gamut of swinging '60s, high-fashion styles fresh off the Paris and London racks, including a mini-dress with oversized, clear acrylic sunglasses, a black patent leather pantsuit, and the famous Paco Rabanne dress of shiny metallic discs.

Audrey felt that Givenchy's clothes had protected her figure and disguised its flaws, allowing her to feel more self-assured. Audrey said in 1966, "I've got this figure of mine that looks impossible in off-the-rack clothes. If the length's right, then the top swims on me. It's very discouraging to see yourself looking practically malformed. I loathe trying on clothes."

At Donen's insistence, however, as reported in the *Ladies' Home Journal* (January 1967), "Audrey braved a tour of *prêt-à-porter* (fashionable ready-to-wear) shops in Paris. After a few hours she stopped short and announced: 'I've had it. You two (referring to her escorts Donen and husband Ferrer) know what's right for me, you do the shopping. I'll try on whatever you bring me. But in a nice comfortable hotel suite.'"

Ferrer and Donen went on a shopping spree the next morning. "We raced through about twelve boutiques like madmen," said Ferrer. "Heaven knows what the salesgirls thought." When later asked by a journalist, a salesgirl said she thought they were indeed a pair of madmen. "I went into the window to put up a new display before the shop opened at nine-thirty, and there were these two American men waiting on the doorstep. One of them insisted on buying practically every item right out of the window and off the walls. The other one kept holding up dresses and yelling across the racks, 'Hey, would Audrey like this?' Whenever they were in doubt about something, they took it." They purchased ninety "ruthlessly youthful" articles of clothing, from which Audrey chose twenty-nine for the scenes that take place in the film's present. For the clothing featured in the film's flashbacks, the director's wife Adelle suggested American designer, Ken Scott, known for his colorful floral print designs and psychedelic juxtapositions of color—a style that would run up against Audrey's self-imposed restrictions on the way she would be dressed. (Forbidden were almost all primary colors, as were "busy" patterned dresses. Swimsuits were to be exactingly padded, yet closely fitted around hips disguised with straight lines.)

Scott would later resign from the film in the midst of production. "From the outset," he said, "Audrey had very firm, not to say rigid, ideas about how she should be dressed. No bright colors (reportedly no reds at all), and above all, no prints. She said they would take away from her face. Can you imagine—Audrey Hepburn, with her head, worried about a dress upstaging her? She was fine about the swimsuits, though. Audrey is, well, a very slim girl indeed, and she agreed right away when I suggested a small amount of padding."

After Scott's resignation, Donen wanted to see still more contemporary items. Clare Rendlesham, the editor of the British fashion magazine *Queen,* who announced "the death of couture" with fictional obituaries of Balenciaga and Givenchy, was called in as fashion consultant. "I gathered together, from London and Paris, some seventy outfits and brought them to Stanley at his hotel," reported Rendlesham. "Audrey flew into Paris from Switzerland, tried on clothes all day, and took the last plane of the day out of Paris back home to Switzerland. I've never seen anything like her professionalism. She's not all that easy to dress, either. The lines have to be just so. She likes all the sweaters and blouses taken in almost like skin. It was very new for her, wearing an outfit that came straight off the peg for only seventeen guineas."

This film introduced other transformations for Audrey—her hairstyle, and even the shape of her eyebrows. Her longtime make-up artist, Alberto De Rossi, whom she credited with creating "the Audrey Hepburn eyes," said, "I modified her eyebrows for this film. Of course, you don't notice. Audrey's eyebrows are twice as thin now as when she made her first film. Then they were immense—but you never noticed how I brought them down, film by film. I've given her completely new eyes for this film. Very, very, subtle."

For the film's period hairstyles, Grazia De Rossi, Audrey's own hairdresser since *Roman Holiday* and wife of Alberto, was standing at the ready. For the modern hairdos, London specialist Patricia Thomas was flown to the set in Paris. About the experience, she said, "It's always a little tricky doing any new customer's hair for the first time, you know. And with someone like Audrey Hepburn who has such a clearly defined image, it was perhaps even more difficult. Audrey was very concerned about keeping a small, neat head. She's right, of course. It suits her perfectly." After trying innumerable styles, four were deemed suitable, and wigs were ordered immediately from Italy.

But Audrey was asked not only to eschew a Givenchy wardrobe and alter her hairstyle, she was also asked to forgo body doubles for scenes shot in bikinis and even to appear nude without the flesh-colored swimsuit she proposed for a love scene. She was self-conscious about her skinny upper body, and particularly about her hips that had broadened after childbirth. It was a difficult compromise for Audrey, worried about being physically exposed to her fans for the first time. Donen reassured her that her body was the envy of most women her age, and she came through on film with a convincing simula-

tion of a person comfortable with her own body image. Not surprisingly, magazine coverage dealt mainly with the exposure of Audrey's legs in very short skirts and her bathing suits with plunging necklines. They also noted that the role called for her to be frequently in bed with handsome costar Albert Finney (seven years her junior).

Making *Two for the Road* was cathartic for Audrey. She warmed up to co star Albert Finney immediately, and enjoyed a playful rapport throughout the making of the film. Donen, veteran of two prior films with Audrey, said that he'd never seen her so alive and uninhibited, speculating that it was on account of "Albie." Rumors of a romance between the costars were naturally rampant in the tabloids. Though the press over the years had consistently clamored with rumors of romances between Audrey and each of her costars, it is likely to be true (up to this point) only in the cases of William Holden, during the making of *Sabrina* in 1953 (before her marriage to Ferrer), and Albert Finney in 1966 (after her marriage had begun to fall apart).

Agreeing to do the film on Mel's advice, following Stanley Donen's insistence upon a modern off-the-rack wardrobe, and being rejuvenated by the youthful charm of Albert Finney had all proved so inspirational that a newly liberated, if somewhat disingenuous Audrey remarked to the *Ladies' Home Journal* in 1966, "Who can afford to dress all the time at Givenchy's? I can't. Really. I get one or two suits from him. Dresses for very grand, gala occasions. But all the time? Oh no. I go a lot to little shops, boutiques, to buy clothes to wear at home. I like the look of off-the-rack clothes. I call them my gay clothes."

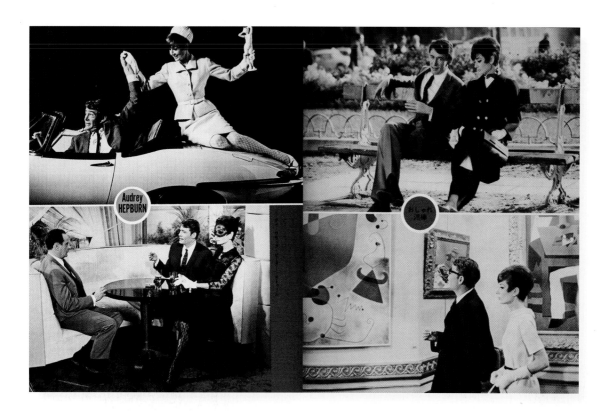

AUDREY HEPBURN SPECIAL, Japan, 1966
Top, bottom, and opposite: pages from Japanese
Audrey Hepburn Special *feature this exquisite*
roundup of many of the Givenchy styles created for
How to Steal a Million.

FILM NEUER KURIER, Germany, 1966
German theatrical program for How to Steal a
Million.

「おしゃれ泥棒」ピーター・オトゥールと

AUDREY HEPBURN SWINGS? YOU'RE KIDDING.

"Well, why not?" asked the movie man. "Garbo talked, didn't she?" He went on to say that in Two for the Road, her new movie for next spring, Miss Hepburn wears mini-skirts, vinyl shorts and also—are you ready?—has a love scene with Albert Finney in which she wears nothing. Nothing. The news was obviously absurd. Audrey Hepburn, as anyone knows, would change her style about as readily as Charles de Gaulle. "Why change?" she once asked a French reporter. "Everyone has his own style. When you have found it, and that is difficult, you should stick to it." Miss Hepburn found hers in 1953 in Roman Holiday, and it has remained inviolate even in The Nun's Story, The Children's Hour, and Breakfast at Tiffany's. Ingenuous, impeccable, jewel-less, Vogue-ish, pure, clean, dignified, vulnerable—add them up, they spell you-know-who. Audrey doesn't need "a look." She is one. She surfaced as one in her twenties and she is still one at 37. If the movie man's report checked out, we decided, there had to be a story behind it. It did, and there was. She told us so herself. "All convention is rigidifying," she said, when we asked her what her metamorphosis was all about. "I think we should try to avoid being rigid—that does age one." Hmm. Well, the whole thing began (continued on page 116)

We knew she had legs, but we'd never seen so much of them. In Two for the Road they'll show from toe to mid-thigh in this English sleep shirt and, in another scene, to bikini's edge.

LOOK AT AUDREY HEPBURN NOW!

LADIES' HOME JOURNAL, United States, January 1967
Interior spread from the magazine. Audrey bravely took the plunge advocated by director Stanley Donen and husband, Mel Ferrer, loosening up her image and going mod.

CINE AVANCE, Mexico, Sept. 16, 1967

SCREEN, Japan, August 1967

JOURS DE FRANCE, France, 1966

SCREEN, Japan, September 1966

ORIZZONTI, Italy, Oct. 2, 1966

SCREEN, Japan, May 1966

SEMANA, Spain, Jan. 25, 1969

Audrey Hepburn– Sexy?

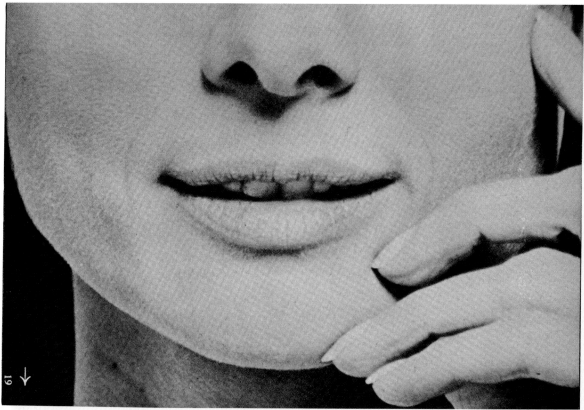

CORONET, United States, November 1966
Opposite and top: pages from Coronet.

CINE AVANCE, Mexico, Sept. 16, 1967
Director Stanley Donen insisted that Audrey forego a body-double for scenes shot in bikinis, even though she worried about being physically exposed to her fans for the first time.

ECRAN, Chile, Oct. 24, 1967

SKOOP, Netherlands, Aug. 10, 1967
Shorts, sweater and ultra-mod vinyl jacket ensemble by Michèle Rosier's V de V.

VIE NUOVE, Italy, Nov. 16, 1967

VANIDADES CONTINENTAL, United States, Mar. 11, 1967

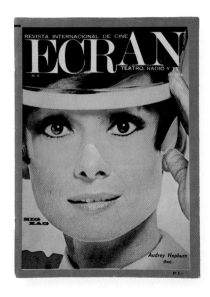

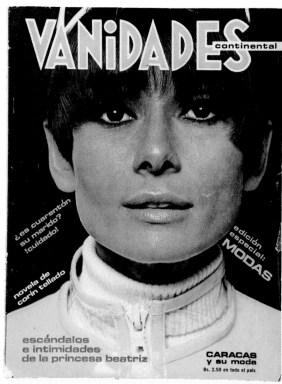

LADIES' HOME JOURNAL, United States, January 1967

Two interior pages from the magazine featuring a range of styles from Two for the Road.

TWO FOR THE ROAD PROGRAM, Japan, 1967

SCREEN, Japan, August 1967

Japan Screen *magazine showcases the space age fashions featured in* Two for the Road. *Here we are treated to alternative angles of Paco Rabanne's famous dress of metal discs. After the shoot, Audrey declared the dress "hurts when you sit in it."*

NUMMER 1–6 JANUARI 1966
Weekblad-Prijs:8F-Ned.50Ct.

Zie
ZONDAGSVRIEND

AUTO-SPECIAAL

ALLE AUTO'S
MET PRIJZEN
3000
KENMERKEN
VAN GADGET
TOT ROLLS

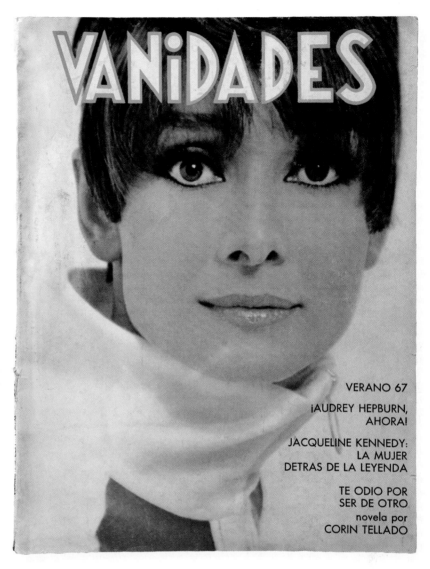

ZIE ZONDAGSVRIEND, Germany, Jan. 6, 1966
Audrey rolls out her campy new image during shooting for How to Steal a Million *in 1965.*

CORONET, United States, November 1966
Coronet *magazine poses a question the press had been asking since the beginning of her career: "Audrey Hepburn—Sexy?"*

VANIDADES, United States, Mar. 26, 1967

AUSTRALIAN WOMEN'S WEEKLY, Australia, Nov. 26, 1975
Audrey stuns in Mary Quant.

ZIE ZONDAGSVRIEND, Belgium, Jun. 30, 1966
1966 brought a departure from the hat-and-gloves look of Givenchy.

MUSIC FROM THE FILM SCORE ALBUM,
United States, 1967
*RCA Soundtrack LP featuring the Henry Mancini score
for* Two for the Road. *Mancini was later grateful that
director Stanley Donen had politely rejected his first
attempt at a film theme, as Mancini (and others) came
to regard his second try as producing the best title theme
of his career.*

TWO FOR THE ROAD PROGRAM, Japan, 1967

LOBBY CARDS, United States, 1967
Two theater lobby cards for Two for the Road *showcasing the autumnal beauty of the film.*

O SECULO ILUSTRADO, Portugal, Aug. 12, 1967
*Audrey recalled that this V de V vinyl slack suit was
particularly uncomfortable.*

OUR WORLD, Israel, Sept. 4, 1967

PROGRAM, Japan, 1966
Top middle and right: Page and cover from Japanese theatrical program for How to Steal a Million.

PROGRAMS, Japan, 1967
Bottom right and left: Page and back cover from Japanese theatrical programs for Two for the Road.

FILM STAR

1967– 1975

to ROMAN HOUSEWIFE

BY 1967, AUDREY'S APPETITE FOR FILM ACTING had reached an all-time low. With the exception of *My Fair Lady*, it had been ten years since Audrey signed on to a film without persuasion. (The last had been *The Nun's Story*, filmed in the winter and spring of 1958.) For ten years, Audrey had performed mostly at the urging of her husband Mel and her manager, and even then only under increasingly complicated terms designed to limit interference with her domestic life.

Audrey's ascension from 1950 to 1954, via *Gigi, Roman Holiday, Ondine,* and *Sabrina,* transformed her from chorus girl to leading lady. (In some markets—particularly California—her name appeared above those of costars Humphrey Bogart and William Holden on the *Sabrina* marquee.) On the ascent, she received Academy, Tony, and New York Drama Critics' Circle awards. Her marriage to Ferrer, in 1954, saw her priorities shift from the professional to domestic, and while Ferrer remained ambitious, Audrey was less and less interested in spending time away from home on her own projects.

The exceptions, *Funny Face* (1957) and *The Nun's Story* (1959), were unique opportunities in different ways: the first to indulge her love of dance (with no less than Fred Astaire), and the second to dramatize experiences under Nazi occupation that were parallel to her own.

By January 1967, at age thirty-eight, Audrey would have been content to step away from public life, but she had already agreed to the Ferrer production *Wait Until Dark*—a commitment made before shooting *Two for the Road.* With rumors rife about troubles in her marriage and an affair with *Two for the Road* costar Albert Finney, Audrey held a press conference at her rented Hollywood home in English "high tea" style, ostensibly to announce *Wait Until Dark,* but also to address rumors. Wearing an orange, angora mini-dress that fell four inches above the knee, she answered questions for two hours about her new hairstyle, short skirts, how happy she was to be in Hollywood, and even a few about the film itself. This interview was one in a series of uncharacteristically frequent interviews Audrey gave at this time, during which she asserted that after almost fourteen years her marriage was a great success, and that Mel was the only man in the world for her. The press wasn't quite persuaded, and in truth, the marriage had become a great disappointment for Audrey in light of her romantic ideals.

Nevertheless, the show went on. *Wait Until Dark* was an adaptation of Frederick Knott's successful Broadway suspense drama centering on the blind wife of a commercial photographer (Audrey) who is tricked into smuggling a drug-filled doll into New York. While alone in her flat, she is terrorized by criminals seeking to retrieve the drugs, about which she knows nothing. Efrem Zimbalist, Jr., plays her photographer husband, and Alan Arkin, Richard Crenna, and Jack Weston are her tormentors.

Once again, Audrey's request for an expensive Givenchy wardrobe was denied. It was judged by Warner Bros. to be unnecessary, even inappropriate for a blind woman confined to her apartment. So, instead, Audrey clothed herself off the rack. No costume designer is credited for this film.

Audrey dutifully researched the part by visiting a clinic for the blind in Lausanne, Switzerland, and she spent several days undergoing blindfolded training alongside real-life trainees at the Lighthouse Institute for the Blind in New York City. Still, those famous eyes were regarded as too expressive to hide behind dark glasses, so she was given contact lenses to help simulate blindness.

Though the film's reviews were mixed, Audrey drew almost unanimous critical praise, including a nomination for Best Actress of 1968, although a number of critics believed that her performance in *Two for the Road* that same year was more deserving of the nomination. Stephen Farber of *Film Quarterly* provided the rare exceptional opinion, "Audrey Hepburn overdoes her cute, artificial vocal mannerisms in the film's early scenes, but she's good in her more hysterical moments."

Judith Crist's review is probably the most even-handed, "If you're not hooked by the well-oiled plot mechanics, you may just see the machinery of a plodding tale of a trio of thugs torturing a blind lady, but if you are grabbed by the vulnerability of charming Audrey Hepburn, as child woman as ever, and by the utter villainy of Alan Arkin—you will wind up screaming in the dark, which is what it's all about."

Wait Until Dark was completed in the summer of 1967. In July, Audrey's doctor confirmed that she was pregnant, but she and Mel had already separated. Ferrer took up temporary residence alone at their villa in Marbella, Spain, before moving permanently to California. In August, Audrey again miscarried, which seemed to bring down the curtain on their marriage. On September 1, 1967, their lawyers announced jointly that the couple were divorcing. The grounds were not officially made public, but privately "irreconcilable differences" were cited.

On November 20, 1968, despite last-minute attempts at reconciliation, Audrey's mother announced publicly that the divorce was final. Some insiders reported that Mel and Audrey's split was primarily caused by his chronic ambitiousness for her career, when she increasingly wanted to be a housebound doting wife and mother. Another aspect surfaced in an interview given by Mel shortly before the separation, in which he revealed some resentment of Audrey's success. He complained of being humiliated in knowing that many people who called him to discuss scripts were really angling to get Audrey's signature on a contract. In 1972, Audrey's comment to journalist and friend Henry Gris for Australia's *Woman's Own Magazine* corroborated Ferrer's complaint: "I thought a marriage between two good, loving people had to last until one of them died. I can't tell you how disillusioned I was. I'd tried and tried. I knew how difficult it had to be (for him) to be married to a world celebrity, recognized everywhere, usually second-billed on the screen and in real life. How Mel suffered! But believe me, I put my career second."

After the separation, Audrey sought to lift her own spirits. One of the first things she did was call upon celebrated French beautician, Alexandre de Paris, who cut and set her hair several times, finally achieving a style that appeared deceptively simple, but which marshaled masterful technique: Each strand was blunt cut, then thinned diagonally with razor from root to tip, then scissor cut on the bias, a sporty new 'do branded by *Vogue* as Audrey's "brisk little mane."

In the summer of 1968, sporting a new look and a new attitude, Audrey accepted an invitation from two friends, millionaire gasoline heir Paul Weiller and his wife, the glamorous Princess Olympia Torlonia, to join them on a cruise of the Greek islands. Among the passengers was a tall, handsome, Italian psychiatrist nine years younger than Audrey, Dr. Andrea Mario Dotti. Dotti's family was on the Italian social registry, and he lived in spectacular wealth in Rome, teaching at the University of Rome and conducting a private practice.

Dr. Dotti was a specialist on the topic of depression, a subject of special interest for Audrey in recent years. Their first discussions were reminiscent of Audrey's inital conversation with Ferrer. In the early 1950s, career was everything to Audrey, and Mel spoke ambitiously about theater and filmmaking. Now, an attractive young psychiatrist was able to discuss matters relevant to her current life circumstances.

As Audrey's courtship with Mel had been quick, so too was her courtship with Andrea. Within six months of their first meeting, and only two months after finalization of Audrey's divorce from Mel, they were married in a civil ceremony at Morges, Switzerland, on January 18, 1969. Audrey wore a pink jersey ensemble from Givenchy, her head wrapped in a matching foulard, and in her hands she held a small bouquet of flowers. Audrey became pregnant in April.

Apart from the possible relationship with Finney and a brief interlude with Prince Alfonso de Bourbon-Dampierre in early 1968, Audrey had felt repressed and inhibited for years. Dotti, a sensual Italian, effortlessly charming, young for thirty, energized her. Without deals to consider, scripts to assess,

and emotions to throttle, for the first time in her life Audrey became extroverted. She embraced her new life, adopting a buoyant, almost careless new spirit. The couple's phone number was listed in the Rome telephone directory, and, seemingly indifferent to paparazzi, she freely shopped and lunched locally with women friends as well as with Andrea.

"I'm in love and happy again," she told Henry Gris in *Woman's Own* (March 1972), "I never believed it could happen to me. I'd almost given up. Now Mia Farrow will get my parts. After all, I worked nonstop from when I was twelve until I was thirty-eight. I feel a need to relax, to sleep in the morning. Why should I resume work and the life I rejected when I married a man I love, whose life I want to live?"

Except for her wedding gown, Audrey momentarily retired from Givenchy, gravitating instead toward youthful boutique wear, such as mini-minis. Though swept up in her new husband's youthful energy, cavorting with him at chic parties and nightclubs all around Italy, Audrey believed Dotti to be "intellectually older" than she. She added that "his education and his work in psychiatry had matured him way beyond his years." But there also loomed a culture gap that Audrey may not have considered, with Dotti apparently subscribing to a canon in which marriage was not the end of male sexual liberty, and in which it was common for married men to keep mistresses. In 1994, Andrea Dotti told *People* Magazine, "I was no angel—Italian husbands have never been famous for being faithful."

During 1969, while pregnant, Audrey retreated to her house in Morges, Switzerland. She remained there after Luca Dotti was born on February 8, 1970. Obliged to his practice, Andrea stayed in their apartment in Rome overlooking the Tiber. Although he visited Audrey each weekend, problems soon developed. Tabloid rumors alleged that Andrea spent his weekday evenings at nightclubs capering like a bachelor. He was photographed with several women, including Daniela, a notorious, jet-setting, rock groupie and one-time consort of the Rolling Stones' multi-instrumentalist Brian Jones. Daniela was a celebrity in her own right, a model featured in the pages of *Vogue* and other European magazines. Audrey couldn't avoid exposure to this negative publicity, extensively covered in the Italian tabloids. It became a taste of what was in store for her thirteen years of marriage.

Drawn back into the world of publicity with resumption of her career in 1975, Audrey was once again obliged to deny rumors of marital problems. Once again, the gossip and speculation was more or less accurate, but it was nonetheless an uncomfortable and humiliating invasion of her privacy. Publicly, Audrey not only defended Andrea's nightclubbing lifestyle, but also attacked the tabloids themselves, in effect accusing them of disingenuous sadism. "Andrea's an extrovert. I'm an introvert. He needs people and parties, while I love being by myself, love being outdoors, love taking long walks with my children and my dogs," she told *McCall's*. "He's done it all his life. It's not as if all of a sudden he's breaking out at the age of thirty-seven to go to nightclubs. It's his way of relaxing, and I think it's important for him to feel free. I don't

expect him to sit in front of the TV when I'm not there. It's much more dangerous for a man to be bored." Audrey also indicted the tabloids for cropping images of Dotti in group situations so that it appeared that he was alone with particular women, saying "Some people find pleasure in the unhappiness of others. If it doesn't exist, they invent it. What can you do? I refuse to answer it."

Years later, Audrey obliquely admitted to having been unfair to the tabloids, clarifying, "My husband and I had what you would call an open arrangement. It's inevitable when the man is younger. I wanted the marriage to last. Not just for our own sake, but for that of the son we had together." Audrey told author Glenn Plaskin in 1992, "Those open marriages don't work. If there's love, unfaithfulness is impossible."

Over the remainder of her marriage to Dotti, from whom she separated in 1980 (their divorce was finalized in 1982), Audrey ceased to make such idealistic claims about marital love. Her declarations increasingly focused upon her two sons. "Ever since I was born I've valued my home life above everything," she told Australian *Women's Weekly* (November 26, 1975). "It's one thing I'm sure of, and the whole point of wanting to be with my children. Once they've been well loved—wisely and well—then whatever life holds for them, they'll have known the security and love behind them. It will be their strength to carry them through life forever."

240

TV, Portugal, Feb. 15, 1968

SCREEN, Japan, February 1968

PROGRAM, Japan, 1968
Japanese theatrical program for Wait Until Dark.

MOVIE NEWS, Australia, February 1968

movie news

BRUARY, 1968. Vol. 4, No. 2

✳ the academy awards story...part 1.✳

Registered at G.P.O., Melbourne, for

ZIE MAGAZINE, Belgium, Oct. 10, 1969

Audrey was one of the few female stars over forty who remained genuinely youthful in spirit, and, significant to her legacy, eschewed trading on sex appeal.

SCREEN, Japan, July 1967

EIGA NO TOMO, Japan, May 1967

INGE ROMAN, Germany, 1968

PROGRAM, Japan, 1968
Top and bottom: Pages from the theatrical program for Wait Until Dark.

ONE SHEET, Spain, 1968
*Another gaffe for Mel Ferrer: his second casting of Audrey, like the first (*Green Mansions, *1959), entirely downplayed her wardrobe. She wore simple, off-the-rack casual wear before the cameras of* Wait Until Dark. *This Spanish poster, far more striking than the U.S. version, emphasizes the primary selling point of the film.*

FIRST, Greece, Nov. 10, 1967
SES, Turkey, Jul. 27, 1968
O SECULO ILUSTRADO, Portugal, Sept. 7, 1968
ROSITA, France, Feb. 20, 1967
ALMANAQUE PLATEIA, Portugal, January 1968

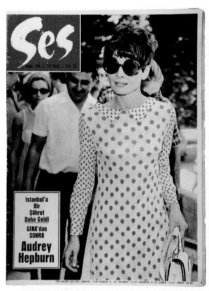

スクリーン

SCREEN

スター・サマー・グラフ／特別読物・夏には
何かが起こる／お楽しみ頁 "プレータウン"

1971

9 特大号

Audrey
Hepburn

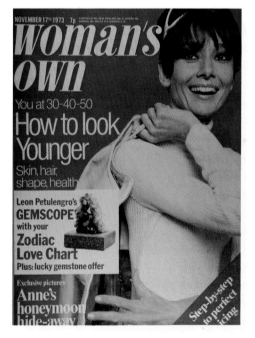

SCREEN, Japan, September 1971

VOGUE, England, Apr. 1, 1971

VECKO JOURNALEN, Sweden, Feb. 18, 1970

WOMAN'S OWN, Australia, Nov. 17, 1973

Audrey looking refreshed and spirited on the cover of Australia's Woman's Own *magazine in 1973 amidst her almost decade-long sabbatical from the film world.*

NR 38 20 SEPTEMBER 1968 KR 1:75 (INKL OMS)
I NORGE 3:85 I DANMARK. 4:45 I FINLAND FMK 2:10

VECKO JOURNALEN

ÅRHUNDRADETS BAL

Jättereportage från
de tusen celebriteternas
fest i Estoril – här
Audrey Hepburn i
sällskap med
Hubert de Givenchy

EXTRA: VALET

sep FOTO: GÖSTA GLASE

VECKO JOURNALEN, Sweden, Sept. 20, 1968
A briefly single Audrey is accompanied by Hubert de Givenchy at a soiree in Portugal, 1968. Translation of the caption adjoining an interior photo of the pair reads, "With a man she remains true to: Hubert de Givenchy."

WEEKEND, England, May 20, 1969
Cover and interior pages of England's Weekend.

MOVIELAND AND TV TIME, United States, May 1969

JOURS DE FRANCE, France, Feb. 8, 1969

ROMAN HOUSEWIFE

1976–1993

to GOODWILL AMBASSADOR

In a sense, Audrey's career as fashion trendsetter ended with *Charade* (1963), and as fashion icon with *Two For The Road* (1967). After *Wait Until Dark* (1968), both filmmaking and public appearance as "Audrey Hepburn," the film star, would be sporadic and, from a fashion standpoint, inconsequential. The colorful youth-oriented styles of the late '60s induced Audrey to take a hiatus from Givenchy couture, but by the middle '70s, and for the remainder of her life, her patronage resumed. But Givenchy had meanwhile adapted his style to contemporary vogue, including transformations not classically "Audrey," now featuring softer fabrics—fluffy cotton instead of gabardine and twill; previously taboo colorful prints with increasingly complex lines; warmer colors—muted beiges, and softly blended pastels replacing the black-and-white and other high-contrast palettes in which a younger Audrey had triumphed during the '50s and '60s.

When Audrey did on occasion return to film, beginning with *Robin and Marian* (1976), it was generally at the behest of old acquaintances, or at times when she felt listless and neglected in her marriage, or just needed a distraction. Finding age-appropriate roles was a challenge. It's tremendously unfortunate that her manager heard too late about the part of an aging ballerina who gives up her career to raise a family, which would have been poignantly semi-autobigraphical for Audrey (the role, in 1977's *Turning Point*, had already gone to Anne Bancroft). Still, the role of Marian—a heroine wishing to recede into comfortable anonymity—held a certain appeal for her, as did the autumnal quality of the script.

During this time, Audrey sought to shake her former Hollywood image of, in journalist Nicolas Freeling's words, "[the] perpetual incarnation of a Roman holiday where the sun always shines and the traffic does not pollute; a rosy glow of innocent, extrovert gaiety." She recognized that while that aura had been her calling card of sorts, it might not serve her as well in middle age or in the new realism in films of the 1970s.

Early in her marriage to Dotti, Audrey had already wished to shed her prim image. She complained to journalist Walter Rainbird in *Weekend Magazine* (May 14–21, 1969):

I'm tired of being thought of as a dear, sweet, not-bad-looking, thin legged, flat chested girl. I'll admit I'm not as well stacked as Sophia Loren or Gina Lollo-whatever-her-name-is. But there is more to sex appeal than just measurements. Those curvy screen sirens don't even know what it is never mind how to use it . . . I don't need a bedroom to prove my womanliness. I can convey just as much appeal fully clothed, picking apples off a tree or standing in the rain, as some of those stars think they do wearing practically nothing. The secret of real appeal is that you must feel it, deep down inside you. It is something that is suggested rather than shown. Take a simple thing like a handshake. I can put more oomph into it than most women can in a walk. When you hold your hand out to a man, you think to yourself, "I'm all woman. I'm all woman." And when your hand touches his—POW! I'm fed up hearing that I'm just "plain Audrey." The truth is that I know I have more sex appeal on the tip of my nose than most women have in their entire bodies. It doesn't stand out a mile, but it's there.

In fact, one purpose of emerging from semi-retirement to do *Robin and Marian* had been to emend her image; but, unfortunately, the hasty Richard Lester direction and the public's lack of interest in the film's reflective, midlife anti-heroics muffled that result. Speaking for all of Audrey's admirers, Howard Kissel of *Women's Wear Daily* wrote, "It has been all too long since we have seen Audrey Hepburn . . . But it seems a cruel joke to have waited eight years to watch her do such dreary stuff. The idea of an anti-heroic Robin Hood seems right for our times, but anti-heroic should really mean more than lugubrious and flaccid."

Audrey wasn't happy with the film either, and it took three years to lure her back to work again. The press continued to report Andrea's alleged infidelities, and director Terrence Young's offer to make *Sidney Sheldon's Bloodline*, a thriller about an heiress whose life is threatened by extortion, somehow struck Audrey as offering a refreshing furlough.

Young, who had also directed her in *Wait Until Dark*, described the challenge of getting Audrey to accept a film role in the late 1970s: "First of all you spend a year or so convincing her to accept even the principle that she might make another movie in her life. Then you have to persuade her to read a script. Then you have to make her understand that it is a good script. Then you have to persuade her that she will not be totally destroying her son's life by spending six or eight weeks on a film set. After that, if you are really lucky, she might start talking about costumes. More probably she'll just say she has to get back to her family and cooking the pasta for dinner, but thank you for thinking of her."

Sidney Sheldon's Bloodline (1979) had no pretensions as anything but a potboiler. Audrey did get to wear Givenchy, though in styles less timeless than had been on offer fifteen years earlier. Reviews of the film were unanimously and justly scathing. *Variety* expressed a sort of protective scorn for the film in Audrey's defense: "Though it would take several pictures on the level of *Bloodline* to seriously damage her stature, it's a shame she picks something like this now that she works so seldom." Audrey's strength had always been to inhabit and elevate potentially thin roles in slick productions, giving them real style and feeling. But, *Bloodline*'s plot was a mess, and too many costars (including James Mason, Romy Schneider, Omar Sharif, Gert Frobe, Irene Papas, and Ben Gazzara) were jockeying for attention.

Shortly before the release of the film, Nicolas Freeling of the *British Telegraph Sunday Magazine* posed a question that was on the minds of many: "Why on earth did she take on this film?" Freeling translated Audrey's answer: "The director (and) the cameraman are old friends, eminent in their profession, and in both of whom she has confidence. The locations were near her home; she could fly to be with her children at every spare moment. She was given great latitude in the contract, and availed herself of it." He himself didn't quite buy it, but speculated that the real story might invade her privacy, which he was reluctant to do. We can conjecture that Freeling had hints of the marital discord that would end in divorce.

There was also the enticement of the twenty-six Givenchy creations she would wear in the film. As Audrey noted in *Woman's Own* magazine that March, "It's a real treat, and I keep the wardrobe. . . ." When asked if this cache helped persuade her to take on the film, she reportedly shrugged in confession.

Audrey described how her style has evolved: "Over the years I've learned to know what's right. Soft clothes, I love.

254

Thank God all those stiff, rigid woollens and taffetas have gone out. Now everything is softer, more feminine . . . I love the fashions now because practically wherever you go, anything goes! Ten years ago I would have hesitated to do my shopping in Rome in a pair of blue jeans. It was very rare to see anyone going around like that." In *Australian Women's Weekly* later that year, Audrey reported, "I love slopping about in jeans and sweaters. Of course, I try to look my best all the time for my husband and children, as well as when we go out more formally."

Audrey knew that *Bloodline* had been substandard, but her disappointment in the film and the doldrums of her unhappy marriage were mitigated by the twinkle-eyed masculine charisma of her costar Ben Gazzara, with whom she became involved, and whom she would follow into a second project, Peter Bogdanovich's *They All Laughed* (1981).

Dotti (from whom she was now separated) was the sensitive and cultivated intellectual type, while Gazzara—born in the United States to poor Sicilian immigrants—was outgoing, energetic, and physical, even cocky. Vincent Canby of the *New York Times* observed when reviewing *They All Laughed*, "Ben Gazzara [plays] in the way of someone who labors under the misapprehension that he is loaded with charm, nothing less than a combination of Bogart, Grant, and Gable." Dotti was a sort of intellectual refinement of what Audrey saw in Mel Ferrer, a philosopher rather than a cultural sophisticate. Gazzara's appeal cut the other way, with an, earthy vitality.

The dalliance wouldn't last. During the production of *They All Laughed,* Gazzara reportedly ended the affair by deliberately parading around the set with younger women friends, which Audrey is said to have (understandably) resented.

Incidentally Bogdanovich, a stickler for realism, asked Audrey to simply wear her own everyday clothing for the film, stressing in his DVD commentary track that her wardrobe consisted of her own personal clothing, which she had brought to New York without expecting to wear it for the production. It included blue jeans, a silk shirt, oversized wraparound shades, and a peacoat. No wardrobe director is credited on the film.

The Gazzara episode suggested to some observers that Audrey was indeed ready to fall in love again. At least that was what Connie Wald, widow of famed producer Jerry Wald and friend to Audrey for almost thirty years, gleaned from the situation. Though Wald was in Los Angeles and Audrey was in New York, she arranged to have Audrey meet her friend Robert Wolders, who was in the city arranging a televised memorial for his recently deceased wife, screen legend Merle Oberon. Wald suggested that Audrey might participate alongside luminaries such as Charlton Heston and Rod Steiger. Wolders phoned Audrey, and the two sparked a friendship. "We liked each other immediately," he explained to Audrey's biographer Charles Higham in 1984. "It was a normal, friendly kind of contact we had, nothing more. I liked her a lot and she really did try to put me at ease. Audrey had known Merle and admired her. She understood her death was a great loss to me, and encouraged me to talk about it."

Wolders and Audrey shared a certain European refinement, range of interests, and tastes. Both also had delicate constitutions. Like Audrey, Wolders had spent the years during World War II in a suburb of Arnhem. Early in their relationship, over a series of further phone conversations, Audrey confided her disappointment in marriage and some of her longings.

Wolders proved to be a doting and ardent companion who inspired in Audrey great joy. Her maternal instinct was awakened by Robert's health complications, including fainting spells, headaches, digestive problems, and other ailments that could be traced back to the privations of life under Nazi occupation (as could Audrey's anemia and other health concerns). By April 1981, while not yet legally divorced from Andrea Dotti, she declared to the press, "I love him [Wolders] and I'm happy."

At this time, Audrey did not know that pieces were slowly falling into place to bring her life full circle. At the time of Holland's liberation in 1945, Audrey had benefitted from the humanitarian hospitality of the United Nations Relief and Rehabilitation Administration (UNRA), the forerunner of the United Nations International Children's Emergency Fund (UNICEF). Audrey had, in turn, participated in UNICEF radio and television appeals as early as 1954. After her second semi-retirement in 1981, she devoted more time to fundraising galas and other events, thanks in part to the support and companionship of by then constant companion Wolders. She would later say, "I could never have worked for UNICEF without Robbie. Apart from my personal feelings, there's just no way I could do the job myself . . . he's the one who gets the flights and the hotels for free when UNICEF can't afford to send me on their budget. He's the one who checks the mikes in the hotel rooms before the press conferences, and he's the one who encouraged me to make it a full-time occupation."

Audrey's only professional appearance between *Wait Until Dark* (1968) and *Robin and Marian* (1976), outside of four one-minute 1971 television commercials shot in Rome for a Tokyo wig manufacturer, was a UNICEF Christmas TV special in 1970 called "A World of Love." In March 1988, at a UNICEF fundraiser in Tokyo, then-director James Grant asked Audrey to step up her participation, essentially succeeding Danny Kaye as Special Ambassador, a celebrity role he created in 1954 and held until his death in 1987. Other celebrities that concurrently and generously donated their time as ambassadors to the cause included Peter Ustinov and Harry Belafonte, and later, Roger Moore and Mia Farrow.

In March 1988, Audrey agreed to work for UNICEF for one year. Over the next three and a half years, until her health precluded it, she traveled the world to draw attention to places in need of help to fight famine and drought—Ethiopia, Turkey, Venezuela, Ecuador, Guatemala, Honduras, El Salvador, Mexico, the Sudan, Thailand, Vietnam, and India.

In 1991, at a retrospective in her honor, Gregory Peck told the audience, "You have not seen the real Audrey until you have seen her in the jungles of Bangladesh, in Thailand, in Vietnam, in the holding camps of the dispossessed world among hundreds of starving people."

"The human obligation," Audrey said in 1992, "is to help children who are suffering anywhere in the world. All the rest is luxury and trivial. . . . My great ambition is to have nothing to do but simply to stay at home, devoting myself to my tomatoes and my roses, looking after my dogs, and one day I'll do it, but not yet, not until I'm sure that I know that 'my children' in all countries are well treated."

Though by this time certain that she had found her true vocation, she was nevertheless lured by director Steven Spielberg to make one last appearance before the cameras. In 1989, she took time off from her role as UNICEF Ambassador to play the small part of a guardian angel, Hap, who welcomes newly dead Pete Sandish (Richard Dreyfuss) to the afterlife in *Always* (1989).

Audrey's last dramatic performances were a series of 1991 UNICEF benefits called Concerts for Life, in which she read from *The Diary Of Anne Frank,* with original music scored, written, and conducted by Michael Tilson Thomas and performed by the London Symphony Orchestra. The performance opened at Barbican Hall in London and toured to Philadelphia, Miami, Chicago, Houston, and New York. "I was exactly the same age as Anne Frank," Audrey explained to reporter Lesley Garner of the British *Sunday Telegraph,* May 26, 1991. "We were both ten when war broke out and fifteen when the war finished. I was given the book in Dutch, in galley form, in 1946 by a friend. I read it . . . and it destroyed me. It does this to many people when they first read it but I was not reading it as a book, as printed pages. This was my life. I didn't know what I was going to read. I've never been the same again, it affected me so deeply."

Some of her work for UNICEF took place at personal risk. It had taken her a year to get funding for her trip to Somalia in 1992. When she finally tried to get a visa, she was told, "There are no visas, because there is no government. You just fly in and hope you won't get shot down."

Upon returning from Somalia in 1992, Audrey told her son Luca, "I have been to hell and back." At that time, the catastrophes of Somalian genocide and refugee camps were little known. At a press conference, Audrey spoke passionately to journalists about her memories of 1945 when the whole world seemed to say "never again," though decades later there were still parts of the world in which genocide was horrifically routine.

Reportedly, Audrey had been suffering abdominal pains in advance of her tour of Somalia, and finally sought medical attention on her return to Switzerland in late October 1992. Exploratory surgery a few days later revealed that abdominal cancer had been spreading from Audrey's appendix for perhaps as long as five years.

Audrey spent the week after the operation recuperating at Connie Wald's in Beverly Hills, her usual California residence, and shortly thereafter began chemotherapy—luckily with minimal side effects. However, within the next week she was also discovered to have bowel cancer. "We had a few days of hope, careful walks by the pool," her son Sean said, "and nights of watching television, all of us sitting on the floor around her bed, watching comedies . . . nature shows . . . she spoke of how much she enjoyed them. They reassured her that the miracle of nature was still well and alive and that life, with its beautiful simplicity, would continue no matter what."

Audrey was back in surgery on December 1, 1992, and within an hour, the surgeon stopped the procedure and told Audrey's family that the cancer had spread to the point of being inoperable. Reportedly, when Sean quietly told his mother that according to the doctor, her condition was beyond surgery, she looked away and calmly said, "How disappointing."

Audrey returned to Connie Wald's for several weeks, then Hubert de Givenchy helped her make arrangements to travel to Switzerland. Before leaving Los Angeles, Audrey said goodbye to Billy Wilder and her other friends on the West Coast. Upon returning to Switzerland, Audrey spent time in her garden each day, but stalked by paparazzi, soon ceased going outdoors at all.

Audrey Hepburn died at home on January 20, 1993, in the company of Robert Wolders, Sean, Luca, Mel Ferrer, and Andrea Dotti. She was buried in Tolochenaz, Switzerland, where people from all over the world sent dozens of flower arrangements.

After Audrey's death, Robert Wolders, Sean Ferrer, and Luca Dotti set up the Audrey Hepburn Hollywood for Children Fund to raise money in her honor for various worldwide children's charities. Sean has been the chairman since its inception in 1994, and the foundation has secured hundreds of Hollywood stars for its advisory board. Robert Wolders said, "Audrey always felt that if she inspired her own children to continue her work, that would be her greatest reward."

Hubert de Givenchy said, "I keep thinking of her funeral. It was so like her, so simple, so fresh, in the presence of all those she had loved, famous or unknown. The whole world was united in tenderness and love. Despite the difficulties of life, Audrey always knew how to preserve in herself a part of childhood. And her magic, she spent her life trying to give it to us. It's that which made her an enchantress, a gentle, inspiring magician of love and beauty. Such enchantresses don't wholly go away."

Over the years, many people who knew Audrey shared sentiments about her. In 1990, designer Ralph Lauren said, "There are two or three people who will remain in the public's eye forever because their appeal is classic and timeless. Audrey Hepburn is No. 1."

Mel Ferrer said to Geoffrey Boca in *Redbook* (July 1956), "She is a natural being in an artificial world. She is honest and without guile. No amount of success will ever change her personality. That's why I fell in love with her."

Designer Michael Kors said to *People Extra* (Winter 1993), "Women wear things today that they just take for granted, but without Audrey Hepburn they probably wouldn't be wearing them."

Photographer and friend Richard Avedon said, "She never had any idea how beautiful she was: Audrey invented chic."

Janis Blackschleger (executive producer of the PBS program *Gardens of the World with Audrey Hepburn*) said in *People Extra* (Winter 1993), "When you were with her you felt prettier, better about yourself and your own possibilities." Finally, Audrey herself said to Curtis Bill Pepper in *McCalls* (January 1976), "I don't care anymore if I don't go around the world, if I don't see more than I've seen. I feel very saturated—in the good sense, not in boredom. I haven't enough time to think about everything I've done and seen. Living is like tearing through a museum. Not until later do you really start absorbing what you saw, thinking about it . . . and remembering . . ."

MCCALL'S, United States, January 1976
Cover and interior spread: During the publicity campaign for Robin and Marian, Audrey would be called on to explain her long absence to a curious public. Several reflective articles and interviews were published at this time.

ILLUSTRATED POLITICS, Russia, Sept. 21, 1976

AUSTRALIAN WOMEN'S WEEKLY, Australia, Mar. 31, 1976

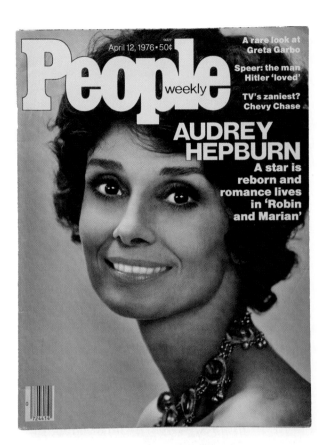

PEOPLE, United States, Apr. 12, 1976

AUSTRALIAN WOMEN'S WEEKLY, Australia, Feb. 28, 1979
Audrey's iconography had been established as youthful, even into her late thirties. Fans and press contemplated her advancing years with trepidation.

WOMAN'S OWN, Australia, Mar. 17, 1979
A sampling of Givenchy's late seventies stylings for Sidney Sheldon's Bloodline.

TELEGRAPH SUNDAY MAGAZINE, England, May 20, 1979
Cover and interior spread.

FILM COMMENT, United States, March–April 1991

COSAS, Chile, Nov. 4, 1991

PARIS MATCH, France, Oct. 17, 1991

Givenchy's last wave of couture for Audrey in 1991.

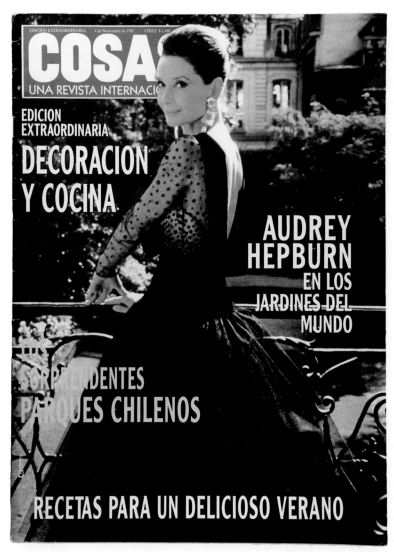

PARADE, United States, Mar. 5, 1989

LA NACION, Argentina, Jan. 31, 1993
Top and bottom right: Interior spread and cover.

PARIS MATCH, France, Oct. 17, 1991
*"Faithful Star" Audrey Hepburn posing with Hubert
de Givenchy for Paris Match in 1991. Their personal
and professional association had endured almost forty
years at this point.*

VANITY FAIR, United States, May 1991

HOUSE & GARDEN, United States, January 1991
*An ardent recreational gardener, Audrey had the plea-
sure of visiting spectacular and palatial gardens all over
the world in her role as host of the 1991 television series*
Gardens of the World with Audrey Hepburn.

FOR THE WOMAN WHO WASN'T BORN YESTERDAY

I T A

THE INTERNATIONAL MAGAZINE FOR WOMEN

THE DIVINE MISS HEPBURN

ISSUE 2 APRIL 1989 ✳ $5.00
N.Z. $7.50 including GST

9 771032 563016

ITA, Australia, Apr. 2, 1989

Audrey featured in candids on the cover of Australian International Magazine For Women with two of the greatest loves of her life: at top with Hubert de Givenchy, and in the middle, with the devoted companion of her last ten years, Robert Wolders.

ELLE, France, Feb. 1, 1993

Audrey's countenance reflecting a renewed purpose. For years preoccupied with a deep love of her own children above all other concerns, she eventually would work on behalf of all children.

PARIS MATCH, France, Feb. 4, 1993

Frail Audrey's later life involved tireless effort on behalf of UNICEF, made possible by the doting and devoted help and support of her constant companion, Robert Wolders.

PEOPLE EXTRA, United States, Winter 1993

PEOPLE, United States, Feb. 1, 1993
Two commemorative People magazines, 1993. The renewal of interest in Audrey was immense, and her currency as an international style icon has only grown since.

ELLE, France, Feb. 1, 1993

VANITY FAIR, United States, May 1991
Audrey strikes a balletic pose on a page from a stunning Vanity Fair tribute, run at the height of Audrey's beneficence for UNICEF.

POSTSCRIPT

AUDREY'S RADIANT AND COMPLEX PERSONALITY injected new (or at least newly public) contradictions into feminine roles on and off screen: strength and vulnerability, wisdom and naiveté, hauteur and humility, glamour and modesty, androgyny and femininity. Intriguingly, her persona was effectively both pre- and post-feminist, although significantly, she neither assumed nor advocated an explicit agenda. But in art and in life, personalities that don't resolve into neatly defined social strictures are the most enduringly fascinating.

In her 2002 book *Growing Up with Audrey Hepburn,* Rachel Moseley presented research on two generations of British women. One group consisted of the mid-1990s teens and twenty-year-olds, whose interviews revealed that Audrey Hepburn represented a "romantic nostalgia," or a "subcultural retro style" which reflected "lost . . . innocence" from the era of "glamour and sophistication." From their remove, this younger generation perceived Audrey's "hats, gloves, and bag" look as "performance," "a romance of perfection" coinciding with the time of their parents' (lost) innocence and conformity.

The second group consisted of women who were adolescents in the 1950s. To these women, who grew up with Audrey as her films were being released, her tomboyishness was important, representing rebellious qualities of feminine self-determination and independence, which gave her later, stylish persona an air of deliberate individualism. These women understood Audrey to be earnest, vulnerable, sincere, and original.

Film Critic Molly Haskell wrote in *Film Comment* magazine (March/April 1991):

> *She was one of the last stars to be nourished by the studio system at its best, a cynosure for the collaborative talents of gifted directors (William Wyler, Billy Wilder, George Cukor, John Huston, King Vidor, Blake Edwards, Stanley Donen), costume designers, cinematographers, screenwriters, lighting technicians who created the proper setting and distance for her mystique. Where once she might have seemed impossibly chic, her style and elegance are a welcome relief after two decades of anti-fashion chaos, a period in which women's styles, or 'looks' ranged from punk and executive to dreary unconcern as a badge of authenticity. We can now look at her style with a fresh eye, see her costumes, her grace and speech as one of a piece with a persona in which surface does not usurp soul, but profoundly conceals its torments until passion breaks forth . . .*

In fashionable and popular culture, Audrey's early-career, gamine style has a founding place in ideal notions of female glamour, style, sophistication, body type, androgyny, and even means of social ascension. She presented a complex personality that appealed to both the traditional and the revolutionary, and in this allowed for new possibilities. And with her inimitable charm and depth of character developed through hard-earned experience she made all this seem effortless and inevitable.

Other factors that contributed to her appeal and influence are her "goodness," established in her choice of film roles;

her humanitarianism; her fashion-forwardness; and her vulnerable, anemia induced thinness, which also gave her a figure ideally suited for delicate couture creations. She was a role model who embodied awakening possibilities for women, on the border of gender differentiation, sporting short haircuts, slim-fitting pants, men's formalwear, turtleneck and three-quarter-length-sleeve shirts, dark glasses, and flat shoes—the last of these in stark contrast to the stiletto heels held as standard for women at the time. The flats worn by Hepburn (and later by Natalie Wood in *West Side Story* in 1961) represent a distinctly feminist evolution, associated, as Moseley points out, with "mobility, action and freedom . . . running and dancing."

Prior to Audrey's appearing on the fashion scene, social sophistication required that young girls emulate older women. Youth was an awkward transitional state that one matured out of as quickly as possible. Audrey fortunately followed a bit of early career advice from Richard Avedon, who suggested that she emphasize rather than try to hide the distinctive aspects of her features. Where her figure was concerned, this meant cinched belts which emphasized her unusual twenty-inch waist, low collars to accentuate the length of her neck, no padding to create the illusion of large-breastedness, and so on. It also meant less reformatory makeup minimalism that tends to impart a naturally youthful glow. Both in and out of her films, Audrey wore only rudimentary makeup, and projected unabashed ingenuous youth. Her early image included notoriously unplucked eyebrows, referred to by the press as her "bat wing" brows; hair cut in simple, easy to maintain lengths and styles; and offscreen clothing devoid of fuss or pretension.

Audrey's screen image also conspicuously lacks overt sexuality. She appeals to girls and women particularly because she showcases a feminine identity that does not trade on sex appeal, but rather on a good, stylish, self-possessed persona. She and Hubert de Givenchy shared the same vision, and she said that her choice of his designs reflected the values of that image, including modesty and "good taste." "Everything about her worked toward a female dignity," wrote Marjorie Rosen in *Popcorn Venus.* Of course Audrey is also attractive to men, but her appeal is in a marked contrast to that of more caricatured contemporary emblems of feminine sexuality, including pneumatic Hollywood sirens Jayne Mansfield, Mamie Van Doren, Ava Gardner, Marilyn Monroe, Brigitte Bardot, and Gina Lollobrigida. Audrey eschewed the '50s fussy femininity, including breast and hip accentuation, foreshadowing the slim and mod Twiggy, Mary Quant, and Biba looks that were to come.

That Audrey's appeal extended to men is attested to by the list of leading men reported to have, at least momentarily, fallen in love with her, including William Holden, Albert Finney, Peter O'Toole, Ben Gazzara, and of course Mel Ferrer. A liner note from The Dave Brubeck Quartet's 1955 Columbia LP *Brubeck Time,* recorded during Audrey's youthful heyday, describes the origin of a sighing improvisational saxophone ballad called "Audrey." Celebrated jazz photographer Gjon Mili happened to be standing in the studio while the recording session was commencing. This exchange is recorded in the liner notes:

'"I would like," said Gjon, closing his eyes and raising his hand expressively, "I would like to see Audrey Hepburn come walking

through the woods—"
"Gee," said Paul (Desmond) wistfully, "So would I."
"One," I said, noticing the glazed expression about Paul's eyes,
"Two, three, four."
And we played it. Hence, the title.

The most significant recurring themes of the Hepburn theatrical persona are those of a Cinderella (*Roman Holiday, Sabrina, Funny Face, My Fair Lady*) and the ugly duckling (*Funny Face, My Fair Lady*). Audrey's personal radiance notwithstanding, her characters' mobility and inspirational/aspirational uplift is surely a part of her appeal.

Upward mobility through dress is explored in all five of Audrey's most influential films, *Roman Holiday, Sabrina, Funny Face, Breakfast at Tiffany's,* and *My Fair Lady*. This theme undoubtedly underlies Audrey's ongoing influence. She is much more than just another pretty model, but rather is a heroine in popular mythologies that show a young woman transformed by fashion into her own feminine paragon—and, yes, finding love along the way. To Audrey's fans who followed her on screen and in fashion and film magazines, the fantasy roles for which she was emblematic—a good and deserving heroine whose innate taste and poise bloom when given the opportunity—were irresistible, and easy to identify with. That the transformations involved high fashion was part of the fantasy, and when the couture was shown in magazines presenting fashion as rarified but attainable, the fantasy reinforced a sense of possibility. That the couture in question was of the "less is more," understated good taste of Givenchy increased the popular sense of identification with Audrey. "Simplicity was her trademark," commented Leslie Caron in *Vogue*, April 1993. "She had the originality never to wear any jewelry, and this at the time of double rows of pearls, little earrings, lots of 'little' everything."

Another aspect of Audrey's enduring appeal lies in the way that her image reconciles some of the apparent contradictions between feminism's desire for liberation and the pre-feminist attraction of more traditional roles and mores. Audrey embodies an innocence and femininity that are expected of a pre-feminist woman seeking romance and marriage, but the way Audrey ends up there—transformation on her own terms—is decidedly feminist in effect. She, and her fans, get to have it both ways.

ACKNOWLEDGMENTS

I would like to thank the following cafés for allowing me to sit and write—sometimes for hours on end—for the price of a cup of coffee, or two:

In San Francisco: Café Trieste on Grant, Momi Toby's on Hayes, Royal Ground on Polk (near Vallejo), and Ritual Coffee Roasters on Valencia.

In Oakland/Berkeley: The French Hotel on Shattuck, Café Trieste on San Pablo, Peet's Coffee & Tea in Montclair, Vault Café on Adeline, and Saul's on Shattuck.

The following books were both helpful resources and are recommended reading: *Audrey Style,* by Pamela Clarke Keogh; *Audrey Hepburn,* by Barry Paris; *Audrey Hepburn: A Celebration,* by Sheridan Morley; *Audrey Hepburn: An Elegant Spirit,* by Sean Hepburn Ferrer; *Audrey: Biography of Audrey Hepburn,* by Charles Higham; *The Complete Films of Audrey Hepburn,* by Jerry Vermilye; and *Growing up with Audrey Hepburn: Text, Audience, Resonance,* by Rachel Moseley.

At Chronicle Books, thanks to Sarah Malarkey for taking a chance on this first-time writer; to editor Steve Mockus for creativity, patience, and flexibility in the collaborative process that brought this work together; to designer Natalie Davis for her visual wit and sincere adoration of Audrey; to Erin Thacker for her reliable and timely follow-through on the production side; to Emilie Sandoz for perhaps the least fun, but in no way least important task of critically eyeballing and fact-checking the details and minutiae, the integrity of which marks the difference between gossip and biography.

Thanks also:

To the gifted Jay Dixon for his luminous photographs (jaydixon.com)

To Pamela McKay for the generosity of her time, materials, and perspective. I recommend viewing her excellent fan site at www.melferrer.com. (Mel, you have a real friend in Pamela!)

To Robert Wolders for enabling Audrey to actualize her late-in-life humanitarian triumphs; and to Sean Hepburn Ferrer for his commitment to his mother's ideals and memory by carrying on with her charitable foundation. (Click "children's fund" at www.audreyhepburn.com)

To Toshiba for their very durable Satellite series of laptops. The text of this book was written on a battered, antique, but still functional model A45-S150 purchased in 2002, whose screen cover in the last months of writing this book was held up by a strip of packing tape.

And finally, thank you to Jennifer, Jessica, Doris, Larry, Joe, and Judy for love, support, and patience with my preoccupation and limited availability during the course of writing this book.